The Glorious Revolution

Titles in the World History Series

The Age of Feudalism
The American Frontier
Ancient Greece
The Ancient Near East
Architecture
Aztec Civilization
Caesar's Conquest of Gaul
The Crusades
The Cuban Revolution
The Early Middle Ages
Egypt of the Pharaohs
Elizabethan England
The End of the Cold War
The French and Indian War
The French Revolution
The Glorious Revolution
The Great Depression
Greek and Roman Theater
Hitler's Reich
The Hundred Years' War
The Inquisition
The Italian Renaissance
The Late Middle Ages
The Lewis and Clark Expedition
Modern Japan
The Punic Wars
The Reformation
The Relocation of the North American Indian
The Roman Empire
The Roman Republic
The Russian Revolution
Traditional Africa
Traditional Japan
The Travels of Marco Polo
The Wars of the Roses
Women's Suffrage

WORLD
HISTORY SERIES ▪ ▪ ▪

The Glorious Revolution

by
Clarice Swisher

Lucent Books, P.O. Box 289011, San Diego, CA 92198-9011

To Audree

Library of Congress Cataloging-in-Publication Data

Swisher, Clarice, 1933–
        The Glorious Revolution / by Clarice Swisher.
                p. cm.—(World history series)
        Includes bibliographical references and index.
Summary: Examines the events leading up to and the political
legacy of the bloodless English overthrow of its monarchy.
        ISBN 1-56006-296-7   (alk. paper)
        1. Great Britain—History—Revolution of 1688—Juvenile
literature.   [1. Great Britain—History—Revolution of 1688.]
I.Title. II. Series.
DA452.S95   1996
941.06'7—dc20   95-31687
                                                            CIP
                                                             AC

Copyright 1996 by Lucent Books, Inc., P.O. Box 289011,
San Diego, California 92198-9011

Printed in the U.S.A.

Contents

Foreword

Each year on the first day of school, nearly every history teacher faces the task of explaining why his or her students should study history. One logical answer to this question is that exploring what happened in our past explains how the things we often take for granted—our customs, ideas, and institutions—came to be. As statesman and historian Winston Churchill put it, "Every nation or group of nations has its own tale to tell. Knowledge of the trials and struggles is necessary to all who would comprehend the problems, perils, challenges, and opportunities which confront us today." Thus, a study of history puts modern ideas and institutions in perspective. For example, though the founders of the United States were talented and creative thinkers, they clearly did not invent the concept of democracy. Instead, they adapted some democratic ideas that had originated in ancient Greece and with which the Romans, the British, and others had experimented. An exploration of these cultures, then, reveals their very real connection to us through institutions that continue to shape our daily lives.

Another reason often given for studying history is the idea that lessons exist in the past from which contemporary societies can benefit and learn. This idea, although controversial, has always been an intriguing one for historians. Those that agree that society can benefit from the past often quote philosopher George Santayana's famous statement, "Those who cannot remember the past are condemned to repeat it." Historians who ascribe to Santayana's philosophy believe that, for

example, studying the events that led up to the major world wars or other significant historical events would allow society to chart a different and more favorable course in the future.

Just as difficult as convincing students to realize the importance of studying history is the search for useful and interesting supplementary materials that present historical events in a context that can be easily understood. The volumes in Lucent Books' World History Series attempt to present a broad, balanced, and penetrating view of the march of history. Ancient Egypt's important wars and rulers, for example, are presented against the rich and colorful backdrop of Egyptian religious, social, and cultural developments. The series engages the reader by enhancing historical events with these cultural contexts. For example, in *Ancient Greece*, the text covers the role of women in that society. Slavery is discussed in *The Roman Empire*, as well as how slaves earned their freedom. The numerous and varied aspects of everyday life in these and other societies are explored in each volume of the series. Additionally, the series covers the major political, cultural, and philosophical ideas as the torch of civilization is passed from ancient Mesopotamia and Egypt, through Greece, Rome, Medieval Europe, and other world cultures, to the modern day.

The material in the series is formatted in a thorough, precise, and organized manner. Each volume offers the reader a comprehensive and clearly written overview of an important historical event or period. The topic under discussion is placed in a broad historical context. For example, *The Italian Renaissance* begins with a discussion of the High Middle Ages and the loss of central control that allowed certain Italian cities to develop artistically. The book ends by looking forward to the Reformation and interpreting the societal changes that grew out of the Renaissance. Thus, students are not only involved in an historical era, but also enveloped by the events leading up to that era and the events following it.

One important and unique feature in the World History Series is the primary and secondary source quotations that richly supplement each volume. These quotes are useful in a number of ways. First, they allow students access to sources they would not normally be exposed to because of the difficulty and obscurity of the original source. The quotations range from interesting anecdotes to farsighted cultural perspectives and are drawn from historical witnesses both past and present. Second, the quotes demonstrate how and where historians themselves derive their information on the past as they strive to reach a consensus on historical events. Lastly, all of the quotes are footnoted, familiarizing students with the citation process and allowing them to verify quotes and/or look up the original source if the quote piques their interest.

Finally, the books in the World History Series provide a detailed launching point for further research. Each book contains a bibliography specifically geared toward student research. A second, annotated bibliography introduces students to all the sources the author consulted when compiling the book. A chronology of important dates gives students an overview, at a glance, of the topic covered. Where applicable, a glossary of terms is included.

In short, the series is designed not only to acquaint readers with the basics of history, but also to make them aware that their lives are a part of an ongoing human saga. Perhaps they will then come to the same realization as famed historian Arnold Toynbee. In his monumental work, *A Study of History*, he wrote about becoming aware of history flowing through him in a mighty current, and of his own life "welling like a wave in the flow of this vast tide."

Important Dates in the History of the Glorious Revolution

1517	1520	1540	1560	1580	1600	1620	1640

1517
Reformation: Martin Luther breaks with Catholic Church

1532
Henry VIII breaks with Catholic Church

1566
Elizabeth I issues Thirty-nine Articles, making official the Anglican Church

1603
Elizabeth I dies; James I becomes king

1604
Hampton Court Conference: James orders new translation of Bible

1625
James I dies; Charles I becomes king

1640
Puritans dominate Parliament

1642
Charles I takes troops into House of Commons; civil war begins between Cavaliers and Roundheads

1646
Roundheads win civil war

1648
Army purges Parliament, creating Rump Parliament

1649
Trial and execution of Charles I; England proclaimed a commonwealth under Oliver Cromwell

1656–1657
Puritans impose strict moral laws

1658
Oliver Cromwell dies and military takes over

1660
Prince Charles is restored as King Charles II

1662–1665
Clarendon Code punishes Catholics and Dissenters

1665
Bubonic plague kills sixty-eight thousand in London

1666
Fire destroys central London

1670
Charles II signs Treaty of Dover with Louis XIV

1673
Parliament passes Test Act, barring Catholics from government or military positions

1678
Popish plot against Charles II suspected

1685
Charles II dies; his brother becomes King James II; two rebellions against James II fail

1660	1680	1700	1720	1740	1760	1780	1789

1687
James II uses Court of High Commission to punish enemies; James issues his Declaration of Indulgence

1688
June
Seven Anglican bishops are tried for seditious libel and acquitted

July
Protestant leaders invite Prince William of Orange to invade England

November 5
William invades England, landing at Torbay in Cornwall

November 15
The earl of Danby takes Yorkshire

November 16
James's soldiers desert

November 19
James collapses

December 12
James tries to escape to France, leaving England without a government, but he is captured; riots begin in London

December 18
William enters London

December 21
James vanishes during night, goes to France

1689
Convention Parliament meets on January 22; in February William and Mary accept Declaration of Right and are crowned king and queen; Scotland crowns William and Mary king and queen in May; John Locke publishes *Two Treatises on Government*

1689–1702
Revolution Settlement redefines relationship between monarchy and Parliament

1694
Mary II dies

1702
William III dies

1776
American Revolution

1789
French Revolution

The Struggles for Power and Religious Freedom

The Glorious Revolution took place in England during the last months of 1688 and the early part of 1689. The revolution is considered glorious because it was fought without a single battle and because a new and more democratic form of government took the place of a despotic, or harsh, king, who was overthrown. King James II, who had been unwilling to work with Parliament and had violated English laws, fled the country once Prince William of Orange, a relative of James, had successfully invaded. Parliament had asked Prince William to invade and help restore the legislature's rightful power. When Prince William arrived on the English shore, parliamentary leaders and the English army went over to William's side. Shortly after that, Parliament offered the crown to William and his wife, Mary, daughter of James II, with the understanding that they work with Parliament. This revolution brought permanent changes to English government and society, and its influence spread far beyond England's shores.

Though short and undramatic, the Glorious Revolution was the culmination of events that developed the first modern democracy. For a century England's Par-liament and monarchs had struggled violently with issues of power and religion until leaders, sick of the bloodshed and conflict, quit fighting and set up a new government that would work toward compromise and unity. The Glorious Revolution is important as a symbol of a new

The Glorious Revolution ended the rule of the despotic King James II and brought a more democratic form of government to England.

beginning that followed the degeneration of old traditions. The reigns of the Stuart kings portray the heated conflicts that led reign by reign toward failure. Forging a democracy out of a monarchy was neither easy nor painless. Fostering religious tolerance out of fear and hatred was equally difficult and painful. The leaders who were responsible for these changes had no modern democracy to use as a guide; they were pioneers.

Tudor Monarchy

At the beginning of the seventeenth century, England's government was a constitutional monarchy. The country was ruled by an absolute monarch whose power was without conditions or limits as long as the monarch complied with the constitution, the collection of the country's laws. An absolute monarch's power was thought to be that of divine right—that is, sanctioned by God, who had originally granted power to ancient kings of the Bible—and the right to rule had been passed down through hundreds of generations. Since 1485 the English monarchs had been members of the Tudor family. The Tudors had, for the most part, wielded their power wisely. The last Tudor ruler, Elizabeth I, who ruled from 1558 to 1603, had gained international respect and the love of her subjects due to her political skill and generosity. After she died, a new dynasty, the Stuarts, ruled England. The reigns of these four Stuart kings led to the Glorious Revolution.

Unlike previous monarchs, the Stuarts ran afoul of Parliament, the legislative body that functions somewhat like the American Congress. Parliament has two houses: the House of Commons, similar to the American House of Representatives, has members who represent the districts throughout the nation. The House of Lords, although similar to the American Senate, is restricted to members of the upper class. Today Parliament makes laws and manages the finances of Great Britain, just as Congress does in America. Under Elizabeth I at the beginning of the seventeenth century, however, Parliament did little but meet when Elizabeth called it to grant her more funds to finance her personal affairs and to pay for the nation's needs. Parliament was seldom involved in its country's affairs because it trusted that the monarch would successfully execute them. Under the Stuarts, however, Parliament and the kings became mired in struggles over power and money.

The reigns of the Stuart kings, therefore, tested the English traditional governmental system in ways it had not been tested for a long time. In 1215 the Magna Carta, England's early constitution, established that the law is above the rule of kings. A monarch who breaks laws of the land can be compelled by force to obey them. Because Elizabeth I was a benevolent queen dedicated to her people, no problems arose during her reign. When Stuart kings acted as if their divine right allowed them to act above the law, Parliament took a more active role to force them to obey the laws. The fourth Stuart, James II, clearly violated his right to power, and he clearly broke the country's laws, a situation Parliament felt compelled to correct according to the Magna Carta. The Glorious Revolution followed.

In addition to the struggles over power and law, England's economic situation brought further conflicts. Under

Because Elizabeth I was a popular and well-respected queen, Parliament allowed her to spend the nation's money even though they knew she was accumulating a huge debt, further worsening England's dreary economic condition.

Elizabeth I England began to accumulate a debt. Elizabeth had spent money to keep the nation strong and to please her subjects, but she took in too little in taxes, and she sold off lands owned by the Crown to pay for her expenditures. Because Elizabeth was popular, Parliament failed to curtail her spending even though members knew the debt was accumulating. When James I became king, he inherited the debt, but he was less popular and less successful at getting Parliament to grant him additional monies, especially for his personal expenses. Lack of funds forced James I and the Stuart kings that followed to try to go around Parliament to attain them. In addition, the debt was forcing social changes. The king and the aristocracy lost economic power because they owed a large debt, and they lost wealth when the queen sold lands. The growing gentry class, made up of small landowners, purchased these lands and gradually accumulated money. The wealth of the gentry class stimulated business and commerce, giving rise to a growing middle class, made up of merchants and traders. As the gentry and middle classes became richer, their members demanded more voice in governing the country. They were no longer content to have their interests governed by a king with lavish personal tastes or an aristocracy that catered to him.

Religious conflicts, however, aroused the most heated emotions and touched a larger number of people than any other issue of the century. These religious conflicts were rooted in the Reformation, which began in 1517. German priest Martin Luther began a religious reform movement that spread throughout Europe. These protesters broke away from the Catholic Church and established Protestantism. Reformers, protesting against the elaborate hierarchy of cardinals, bishops, and priests that governed the Catholic Church, believed that individuals could find personal salvation through the Bible. Another key event was the break with the Catholic Church in England. In 1532 Elizabeth I's father, Tudor king Henry VIII, severed all ties with the English Catholic Church and the pope in Rome and declared himself the head of the church. This act established a new state religion in England, the Protestant Church of England, or Anglicanism. Henry VIII took the action because the pope had refused to approve the king's petition for a divorce from Catherine, who had not produced a male heir to the throne. As absolute monarch and head of the church, Henry VIII was free to make his own rules and marry Anne Boleyn. The Reformation also led to another protest movement in England. Those who felt the Anglican Church was too much like the Catholic Church in its structure and ritual broke away and established Puritanism. By the end of Elizabeth's reign the remaining Catholics, the Anglicans, and the Puritans were often in serious conflict with one another.

Finally, and more subtle than any other issue, a different intellectual outlook was emerging. In the past most people explained the world and its events according to their religious beliefs. Everyday happenings were considered part of God's order. But new views were beginning to develop, especially in the universities. During the second half of the seventeenth century, educated people emphasized reason and observation as tests for reality, or truth. These changes affected England's politics.

The Settlement

Under the last Stuart king conflicts reached a point of no solution, and passions over issues became so intense that leaders in Parliament feared a civil war might break out. In a combination of careful planning and bold decisions, English leaders and Prince William led England into the Glorious Revolution of 1688. The revolution led to a number of acts regarding finances, the army, religion, and power. Taken together as the Settlement, these laws constitute a reorganized government that has served England to this day. The Settlement also produced new institutions and procedures to improve and maintain a representative government. The Revolution and its Settlement brought England more than two hundred years of peace at home. Without war and fighting, the nation grew into a rich, powerful, and vast empire.

An artist's depiction of Prince William's landing in England, the event that set the Glorious Revolution into full swing.

British historian George Macaulay Trevelyan thinks that *sensible* might better describe this revolution than *glorious*. Another British historian, Maurice Ashley, sums up the importance of the Glorious Revolution this way:

> The "Glorious Revolution" of 1688 was a decisive event in the history of modern Europe and also of the English-speaking world; for it changed the character of English government, gave meaning to a political philosophy and contributed to the working out of a balance of power among nations. . . .

Traditionally it has been presented as a triumph for the purity of constitutional law over a blatant and outrageous attempt at its perversion, a reaffirmation of the liberties of the English people after the exercise by a monarch of unbridled arbitrary power. . . . But to other twentieth-century historians it has appeared as a "respectable revolution."[1]

Whatever adjectives one uses to describe it, this revolution was unusual for its lack of violence, its short duration, and its part in laying the groundwork for democracy.

1 From Tudor Harmony to Stuart Conflict, 1603–1640

The nearly fifty-year reign of Queen Elizabeth I pleased the English people. An adept leader, she inspired her statesmen to govern with painstaking care for the people. She knew how to be popular and mastered the people's feelings. She blended grand pageants with personal touches. On elaborate progresses, or visits, into the country, for example, she joked with fish sellers, complimented the village singing teacher, and thanked actors for performances in her honor, making each one feel her special affection.

Besides her immense personal popularity, Elizabeth had the advantage of reigning over subjects whose social traditions and hierarchy had been stable for a long time. England was a nation with rural villages, small towns, and one large city, the capital London, which had about 200,000 residents. It was a society that accepted its rigid social classes based on family heritage and land ownership. The nobility, or aristocracy, had both family name and large holdings of land. The gentry owned land and could afford fifteen or sixteen servants, while yeoman farmers had less land and only one or two servants to help with farmwork. Peasants and servants owned nothing and worked for the landed farmers and wealthy nobles. Regardless of class, the social order was patriarchal; that is, the word of the father was law for his wife and children. This traditional economic and social order brought stability to people in country and city alike.

The English people lived in relative harmony during the reign of Queen Elizabeth I, a benevolent and beloved ruler.

Elizabeth's Strategies to Secure Power

Elizabeth used her popularity and the people's goodwill to govern England with autocratic rule, that is, rule by a single person. She declared that the monarch was the supreme governor in all matters. Clergymen, lawyers, teachers, university graduates, and magistrates—all employees of church and Crown—had to take an oath declaring the monarch supreme. To gain additional support for her power, Elizabeth used religion to serve her political purposes. Because she thought a state church would further insure a stable society, she made the Anglican Church the official Church of England and ordered Anglicanism practiced in every village, town, and city. She enforced this structure, even though it denied freedom to Catholics and persecuted Puritans. She abolished Catholic mass and required all English people to attend Anglican Sunday service or pay a fine for the poor. She introduced a book of liturgy, or rites, for religious services, the *Book of Common Prayer*, and made it the law for religious worship, forbidding all other religious ritual. She established a governing body, the Court of High Commission, to make all religious decisions and to make all appointments to church positions. To govern all the clergy of England, she established an official creed, or set of religious beliefs, explaining Anglican theology, called the Thirty-nine Articles. Since Elizabeth viewed religious dissent as political revolt, Catholics, who comprised more than half of the total population, were arrested, with some executed, some exiled, and many fined when they disobeyed. But

most Catholics complied with the laws even though they disliked doing so.

Late in Elizabeth's reign three religious faiths—Catholicism, Anglicanism, and Puritanism—were in conflict over beliefs and entangled in politics. The Puritans represented a large and noisy minority within the Anglican Church. They got their name because they wanted to purify the Anglican Church by simplifying the ritual prescribed in the *Book of Common Prayer* and by giving less authority to bishops chosen by the Court of High Commission. Puritans called the *Book of Common Prayer* a book picked out of a Catholic dunghill because they thought, like Catholic ritual, it imposed too much ceremony between the Christian soul and God. The Puritans also believed individuals had the right to interpret the Bible themselves by their own reading. Elizabeth I, who resented Puritan beliefs more than she resented Catholic practices, encouraged Anglican bishops to suppress Puritan pamphlets and silence Puritans in church. Though they did not revolt, the political propaganda against the Puritans caused many of them to move to Holland and America.

The Arrival of James I

When Elizabeth died in 1603, leaving no heir, Parliament called James VI of Scotland to become James I of England. He began his reign with several handicaps. He followed a beloved queen, but he lacked her magnetic appeal and, as a Scot, her knowledge of English social customs. He faced the large debt and a weak military left by Elizabeth. And he arrived in the thick of religious conflicts. Nonetheless, he made no effort to conserve money or to charm his subjects. To deal with the debt and his personal expenses, James supplemented his allotment from Parliament by selling titles, like lord and lady, to wealthy members of the gentry who had no titles by birth, a practice that offended the aristocracy, who wanted titles limited.

Aware of the religious feuds, James had a dream of healing them, but most of his efforts failed. To appease the Catholics, he resumed relations with the pope in Rome. This action angered Anglicans and misled Catholics, who had assumed they would be free of Elizabeth's religious rules. When Catholics failed to gain their expected rights, a few plotted to kidnap James to get him to promise toleration, but the plot was never carried out.

To help the Puritans, James called the Hampton Court Conference in 1604 to attempt changing the rules Elizabeth had laid down and allow Puritan clergy more freedom. But this action also angered the Anglicans, and the powerful Anglican bishop Richard Bancroft demanded that all ministers conform to the Thirty-nine Articles. Although the conference failed to gain toleration for Puritans, James did succeed in satisfying one of the Puritans' requests, ordering a new translation of the complete Bible, known since as the Authorized, or King James, Version. James had clearly underestimated the intensity of religious hatred and warfare; Puritans hated Anglicans, Anglicans hated Puritans, and both hated Catholics. Yet, as the new king he had to uphold the laws, and enforcing them meant he had to punish all dissenters who broke church rules.

James's underestimation of the depth of religious conflict matched his overall

James I, who began his reign with a large debt and a weak military, also faced mounting religious conflicts throughout England.

lack of understanding of English traditions and mores. He had little tact or charm, speaking to members of the House of Commons in a scolding manner. His interest in theory and his ineptitude with people earned him the epithet "the wisest fool in Christendom." Historian Maurice Ashley said, "He could criticize a theory, but he could not judge a man."[2] In manners and appearance he struck the English as undignified and lacking refinement. He had a shuffling walk, a feature that prompted one historian to observe that James did better when he stayed on a horse. James had a passion for hunting, a sport of which the English approved, but

The Character of James I

In his book The History of England, *historian David Hume, who wrote in the eighteenth century, describes the character of James I.*

"While he endeavoured, by an exact neutrality, to acquire the good-will of all his neighbours, he was able to preserve fully the esteem and regard of none. His capacity was considerable; but fitter to discourse [converse] on general maxims [principles] than to conduct any intricate business: His intentions were just; but more adapted to the conduct of private life, than to the government of kingdoms. Awkward in his person and ungainly in his manners, he was ill qualified to command respect."

he indulged in hunting with the same excess that he indulged in his other pleasures. As his reign wore on, he attended less to government and more to his own entertainment. He drank to excess, and his court parties became more corrupt. In his later years his body grew prematurely old from too much rich food and strong drink, and his behavior became more foolish. He developed an affection for young men, in particular one named Robert Carr. Historian William McElwee describes James's public behavior:

> He appeared everywhere with his arm round Carr's neck, . . . lovingly feeling the texture of the expensive suits he chose and bought for him, pinching his cheeks and smoothing his hair. . . . There could have been few who did not find them ludicrous and unseemly.[3]

From the beginning of his reign, James I and Parliament were at odds. Having exercised little power under Elizabeth, Parliament now sought to gain more control. Members asserted their right to freedom of speech when they differed with the monarch; they wanted to dictate religious and foreign policy; and they planned to initiate legislation. These demands, however, ran headlong into James's perception of his own power. James ardently believed in the divine right of kings. It was true that tradition had long permitted the monarch to govern by divine right, to use inherited prerogative, or privileged, powers that could not be questioned, to take any action necessary for the safety of the state, and to order the arrest of any person thought dangerous, without the usual processes of law. But tradition had also accustomed members of Parliament to be given a certain respect and consideration—at least to be charmed and flattered, not intimidated and insulted. In a 1609 speech James insulted Parliament when he told the members that just as God has power to create or destroy, make or unmake his subjects at his pleasure, so too does a king have power to make or unmake his subjects, to raise them up or cast them down. James believed that he had the power of life or death over his subjects and that he was accountable not to the people, but only to God. This arrogance and blunt speech offended Parliament.

Angered both by the king's poor social behavior and by his arrogance, Parliament acted more boldly. Parliament denied the king money and demanded that he abolish traditional ways of raising funds for himself. Parliament also increased its power by staging its own debates on freedom of speech. In a break from the past, the speaker, or presiding officer, told James that only Parliament could pass laws. In a direct affront to James's wish to downplay religious conflicts, the Anglican-controlled Parliament intensified laws against Catholics, barring them from the practice of law and medicine, forbidding them to travel more than five miles from home, and requiring them to take an oath denying the pope's power to remove rulers. Largely due to Parliament's actions, by 1618 more than twenty priests had been executed, and thousands of Catholics were in jails. According to historians Ariel and Will Durant, "the House defined its rights in bold disregard of James's divinity."[4]

James became equally offended by Parliament's actions and tried to circumvent Parliament by using his own ways of asserting power. He called Parliament to assemble only when he wanted a supply of money, and he prorogued, or dismissed, it when he did not like what happened. He went on spending money on lavish entertainment. When Parliament refused to grant him money, he borrowed from wealthy citizens and increased his debt. Though Commons had passed strict laws regarding religious practices and participation, James refused to enforce them. A combative atmosphere developed between James and Parliament.

Parliament wanted to manage foreign affairs, but in reality foreign policy fell to James, who took few initiatives. Preferring peace and lacking ambition to dominate other nations, James kept England out of war, and the country prospered as a result. He tried to make a stronger union between England and Scotland, but the English Parliament, prejudiced against Scots, defeated the plan. James put most of his foreign policy effort into forming an alliance with Spain, a Catholic country. Given his secret, favorable attitude toward Catholics, he could have gained support from a Catholic country. His direct purpose for a Spanish alliance, however, was to arrange a marriage between his son, Prince Charles, and the Spanish infanta, or princess, Maria, sister of Philip IV, but the two kings could not agree on terms, and the plan failed. His overtures toward Spain, though unsuccessful, brought into the open suspicions among English leaders that James I favored Catholics.

The Decline of James I

During the ten years between 1611 and 1621, when James had tried to govern England without Parliament, he and his reign declined. During that time his wife died, and his health and his wits degenerated. He preoccupied himself with luxury, wild feasts, and drunken horseplay. His debts rose, and he lacked a coherent policy at home or abroad. After the effort to marry his son to the Spanish infanta,

Maria, he looked more like a fool than ever. When Parliament met in 1621, the Commons refused to grant him any more money. James sank fast during the last three years; though he was preoccupied with a few pleasures, he had convulsions, fainting fits, tantrums, and crying spells. He died on March 27, 1625.

Either by redirecting attention to other accomplishments that took place or by affording the king a degree of sympathy, modern historians have treated the reign of James I less harshly than his own Parliament did. In general, historians credit the reign as a time of peace and prosperity. According to historian Maurice Ashley, "we should remember it [the reign] chiefly as the epoch of Shakespeare and [Francis] Bacon at the fullest of their powers—and of the good ship *Mayflower*, which sailed with its load of Puritan emigrants to America in 1620."[5] Historians Ariel and Will Durant call James a better king than others who had more "vigor, courage, and enterprise. . . . He was neither philosopher nor fool. He was only a scholar miscast as a ruler, a man of peace in an age mad with mythology and war. Better the King James Bible than a conqueror's crown."[6]

Charles I: The Second Stuart King

The next Stuart monarch, Charles I, son of James I, reigned from 1625 to 1649. Charles I, who had inherited the throne when he was twenty-five years old, behaved much more in keeping with English social taste. Unlike his father, Charles I cared little for feasting and drinking and pre-

ferred a studious life. According to historians Ariel and Will Durant, he excelled in mathematics, music, and theology, learned some Greek and Latin, and spoke French, Italian, and some Spanish. He loved art, collected paintings, and supported artists, poets, and musicians. He had a reputation as a proud and handsome king, evidence of which appears in the portraits of him painted by Flemish painter Van Dyck. Nineteenth-century historian Thomas Babington Macaulay says of Charles:

> He had received from nature a far better understanding, a far stronger will, and a far keener and firmer temper than his father's. . . . It would be unjust to deny that Charles had some of the qualities of a good, and even of a great, prince. He wrote and spoke, not, like his father, with the exactness of a professor, but after the fashion of intelligent and well educated gentlemen. His taste in literature and art was excellent, his manner dignified, though not gracious, his domestic life without blemish.[7]

Historians Ariel and Will Durant call Charles a "tragic" king who was "a reasonably good man—a loving son, an unusually faithful husband."[8]

Despite his classical education and his reputation as an upright husband, Charles, nonetheless, possessed features that aroused suspicion. The English, who feared French military power and hated French Catholicism, were uneasy when Charles married a French Catholic woman two months after becoming king. His new queen, Henrietta Marie, was the fifteen-year-old daughter of Henry IV of France.

Charles I, depicted as a stately and handsome king by Van Dyck. Though Charles's classical education appealed to English social tastes, his Catholic sympathies aroused suspicions from the Puritan English.

Moreover, Charles was friendlier to Catholics at home than his father had been, and he more strongly opposed Puritans, who had now gained three-fourths of the seats in the House of Commons. Like his father, he believed in his divine right to absolute rule. He believed that a king can make and administer laws, override Parliament's laws, and rule with or without Parliament. In addition, beneath his polished social manner, there appeared weaknesses in his character. British historian Maurice Ashley says of Charles:

His lack of insight and humour, his customary curtness [abruptness] and his intellectual shortcomings were poor protection against the coming storms. He was guided by sentiment and prejudices, he was shifty and unstable; and he usually surrendered himself to advisers of second-rate capacity.[9]

The King's Use of Absolute Power

In volume one of his book The History of England *nineteenth-century historian Thomas Babington Macaulay describes the way Charles I used the Star Chamber and the Court of High Commission, the monarch's judicial bodies, to command power.*

"Foremost among these courts in power and in infamy [disgrace] were the Star Chamber and the High Commission, the former a political, the latter a religious inquisition. . . . The Star Chamber had been remodelled, and the High Commission created, by the Tudors. . . . They displayed a rapacity [forcefulness], a violence, a malignant energy, which had been unknown to any former age. The government was able . . . to fine, imprison, pillory, and mutilate without restraint. A separate council which sate [sat] at York . . . was armed, in defiance of law, by a pure act of prerogative [privilege], with almost boundless power over the northern counties. All these tribunals insulted and defied the authority of Westminster Hall [Parliament], and daily committed excesses. . . . We are informed . . . that there was hardly a man of note in the realm who had not personal experience of the harshness and greediness of the Star Chamber, that the High Commission had so conducted itself that it had scarce a friend left in the kingdom."

Conflicts Between Charles I and Parliament

Given his personality and character alone, Charles could have had a compatible relationship with a traditional Parliament comprised of Anglican aristocrats. However, as Charles asserted his belief that he had absolute power, as Puritans in the House of Commons became more powerful, and as the House of Lords sought to preserve the Church of England, struggles over money, power, and religion intensified, and conflicts rose to new heights.

Each new action appeared to be a reaction to an opponent's previous action, each time escalating the conflicts by steps.

One conflict developed over the monarch's right to call and dismiss Parliament. Between 1625 and 1640 Charles called five Parliaments to ask that funds be granted. When he failed to obtain what he wanted, he dismissed Parliament, sometimes after only a few months in session. When Charles dismissed the third Parliament, the members refused to go, and the speaker introduced three resolutions concerning taxes and Catholics, which Parliament passed. Outraged that Parliament had usurped his authority, Charles prepared to send army troops to enforce his order for dismissal. Parliament adjourned, but Charles punished ten members by having them imprisoned. After that experience Charles ruled without Parliament for eleven years, the longest period in English history without a meeting of Parliament. During the fifth Parliament, called in 1640, hostilities became so intense that the two opposing sides began lining up military troops.

Another conflict developed over the power to control money. Because James I had squandered funds Parliament had granted, Parliament was determined to prevent Charles from doing likewise. Throughout Charles's reign, Parliament

Charles sits at the head of a Puritan-dominated Parliament. After numerous conflicts over power, money, and religion, Charles dismissed Parliament and ruled without it for eleven years.

The Frenzied Climate in London

Eighteenth-century historian David Hume describes the inflamed atmosphere in London that resulted from the battles between Parliament and the king. This excerpt comes from The History of England.

"The nation caught new fire from the popular leaders, and seemed now to have made the first discovery of the many supposed disorders in the government. . . . The capital, especially, being the seat of parliament, was highly animated with the spirit of mutiny and disaffection. Tumults were daily raised; . . . and every man neglecting his own business was wholly intent on the defence of liberty and religion.

The harangues of members, now first published and dispersed, kept alive the discontents against the king's administration."

passed more laws to control money, and Charles became more determined to exercise his divine right to make his own rules to tax and spend. Parliament began by requiring a committee to oversee the king's tax levies, or collections, and his expenditures. Then Parliament changed the tradition of granting the king for the duration of his reign the right to levy export and import duties, called the Tonnage and Poundage Bill. The new law restricted the right to one year. When Charles needed money and Parliament refused to pass a new tonnage and poundage bill, Charles ordered agents to collect the duty anyway and to seize goods from merchants who refused to pay. Further, he asked some citizens for free gifts and ordered a forced loan from all taxpayers: 1 percent of the value of their land and 5 percent of the value of their personal property. He ordered wealthy opponents of his plan to be jailed; the poor ones he ordered into the army and navy. Parliament responded in 1628 with the Petition of Right, a bill requiring approval of Parliament before any tax could be collected. The petition also stated that Charles violated law dating back to the Magna Carta when he forced citizens to give him loans. During the period without a Parliament, Charles continued his financial program in spite of the petition. Finally, he created a new tax; he required coastal cities to pay to have ships protect them and to outfit the vessels in times of peace as they had in the past during times of war. He collected this tax, known as ship money, for many years and rebuilt the navy. All of his actions defied traditional English laws.

A Struggle for Power

Another conflict began over religion and escalated into general war over power. During the period without a Parliament,

Charles imprisoned religious and political opponents. To make his authority more absolute, he made arbitrary arrests and denied prisoners the right of habeas corpus—the right to appear before a court—and trial by jury. He required the Star Chamber, the king's council to try political offenders, and the Court of High Commission, the king's council to try religious offenders, to use more severe punishments. In the spring of 1640 Charles acted to impose strict Anglican rules on Presbyterians in Scotland, but they refused to comply and secretly tried to get help from France. When Charles called on Parliament to send soldiers against the Scots, Parliament refused to grant funds and instead made an alliance with the Scots. Charles called the Parliament traitorous and dismissed it. In this chaotic situation, riots broke out in London, and a mob tried to kill the Anglican archbishop.

By this time Puritans had gained control of Parliament. Fierce battles erupted between the Puritan majority on one hand and the king and his Anglican supporters on the other. This Puritan Parliament accused one of Charles's appointees, the earl of Stafford, of a secret Catholic plot and demanded his execution. It passed severe acts against the Anglican Church that caused destruction of images, stained glass, altar rails, statues, and pictures in Anglican churches. It passed the Exclusion Bill, which excluded Anglican bishops from Parliament, where they had traditionally been members in the House of Lords. It passed rules about its own times to convene and dissolve. It reformed taxation and the jury system. It abolished the king's judicial bodies, the Star Chamber and Court of High Commissions. It ended the king's right to control tonnage

and poundage and to levy ship money. Charles responded by compromising on a few issues, but he insisted on many of his rights and asked for funds. Parliament responded by proposing a militia bill, giving Parliament control over the army. By defying many traditions, the Puritan Parliament tried to shift power from the king to Parliament. Not all members of Parliament, however, agreed with the actions of the Puritan majority.

Movement Toward Civil War

On January 3, 1642, Charles indicted, or accused, five leaders in Commons on charges of treason and took three hundred soldiers when he went in to arrest them. Since the men had gone by the time the soldiers arrived, there were no arrests. In this hostile atmosphere Charles sent his queen to France, and he went to Hull and York in the north. Thirty-five peers from the House of Lords and sixty-five members from the House of Commons remained loyal; they seceded from Parliament and joined Charles at York. This action marked a division between those loyal to the king and those who opposed him. This division also marked the beginning of political parties in England. On June 2, 1642, the remaining men in Parliament gave Charles nineteen propositions that he had to accept to have peace. Charles rejected them, and Parliament voted to raise its own army. Puritan leader Oliver Cromwell recruited and organized volunteers. Parliament succeeded in raising an army by lying; the propaganda told

Charles demands the arrest of five members of Parliament accused of treason. The continuing hostility between Charles and Parliament ultimately resulted in Parliament dividing into two opposing factions.

the people that Parliament was preparing for a Catholic uprising and warned that if the king won, Protestants would be massacred. Parliament's army seized the king's military supplies at Hull on August 17. Ten days later the two armies met at Edge Hill, to start a civil war that would last four years. Religion, power, and money were at the root of the conflict. When the war came, the Puritan classes fought against the king and the traditional aristocracy that continued to support him.

2 From Civil War to Anarchy, 1640–1660

The legislation passed by the Puritan majority in the fifth Parliament and Charles's refusal to accept the limitations it placed on his power put the king and Parliament in direct conflict with little means for peaceful resolution. In 1640 English government had none of the democratic forms that prevent conflicts or resolve them when they do occur. It had no constitution that spelled out the powers of the legislative, judicial, and executive branches of government, a structure that ensures that no branch gets too much power and maintains balance. Without that structure Parliament, which was the legislative branch, and the king, which was the executive branch, tried to acquire more power, and each used the judicial branch to intimidate the other. Although England had never had this kind of democratic structure, conflicts were not threatening as long as Parliament and the people accepted the traditional role of the monarch and the monarch ruled with generosity, as Elizabeth had.

By 1640 more had changed than the growing discontent over the Stuart kings' personal manners and use of power. Puritan leaders had become more daring in their challenge to the traditional Church of England and the king, a change that seemed to inspire their determination to rule. Fueled by new thinking, the rising gentry and middle classes harnessed their economic resources into economic power. Thus, "it was a real shifting of economic power within the community that made civil war possible," according to historian Maurice Ashley. He goes on to say: "What is clear is that the Crown was relatively poorer than it had been say a hundred years earlier and consequently weaker. Therefore the Stuart monarchy and its methods of raising revenue were open to attack by well-to-do critics."[10]

Choosing Sides

Under these circumstances war became inevitable, and Parliament and the king each gathered supporters. Each side had a mix of people who, for some personal or philosophical reason, rallied to their favored side. Individual families often suffered divisions when some members remained loyal to the king and others joined Parliament. Parliament's side had the support of Puritans; the majority of people in London, the seaports, and the manufacturing towns in the south and east of England; the middle class and part of the gentry; the navy; the Scots; three

With support from Anglicans and most Catholics, Charles declares war on Parliament, pitting the Royalists against Parliament's Roundheads.

hundred members of Commons and thirty peers, or members, in Lords; and one writer, John Milton. This side was called the Roundheads, a name acquired from Puritan men, who wore their hair cut short, displaying the shape of their heads. The Roundheads had several leaders: Robert Devereux, earl of Essex; Puritan Oliver Cromwell; and Lord Ferdinando Fairfax and his son Sir Thomas.

The king's side had the support of Anglicans and nearly all Catholics; the majority of people in the university towns of Oxford and Cambridge and the cities in the west and north of England; England's old aristocratic families and a few peasants; the king's army; the Irish; 175 members of Commons and 80 peers in Lords; and most poets. These supporters were the Royalists, also called the Cavaliers. The Royalists had two leaders, Prince Rupert, the twenty-two-year-old son of Charles's sister, and the marquis of Montrose. While Parliament had wealth, Charles, who had no funds granted by Parliament and was prohibited from borrowing money, had to depend on gifts from wealthy estates to finance his military operations.

At the outset of the war in 1642, the Roundheads and the Royalists were evenly matched. The two sides, somewhat like the North and the South in the American Civil War, fought battles in fields and on hills. Both sides had trained officers, but neither side had generals to manage large-scale strategies. The king's navy went over to Parliament's side, and its sailors controlled ports and charged custom duties to fund Parliament's army. Each side had a cavalry. Because a cavalry was the decisive weapon of the seventeenth century, victory in battle went to the side that fought best with horses. Parliament had its headquarters in London, and Charles made Oxford his headquarters. Much of the fighting occurred in the countryside around Oxford, but other battles took place in outlying areas. When the two armies fought in a field, the defeated army retreated to regroup. The victors either pursued the losers or gathered to launch a new offensive.

The king's side won most of the battles in 1642 and 1643. But Cromwell developed into an effective leader with a strong cavalry force. Midway through the war, the Scots joined the Roundhead army. After several Parliament victories between the fall of 1643 and the summer of 1645, Cromwell surrounded Oxford and, with Fairfax, defeated the king's soldiers. In the fall of 1645 the Royalist leader Rupert surrendered, and in May 1646 Charles surrendered, and the war was over.

The End of the War

The war may have been officially over in 1646, but peace had yet to be attained, a difficult task since feelings still ran strong among many different groups. After the war Charles fled to Scotland, where he thought he would be safe and thought he was still acknowledged as king. He also thought that the Roundheads would fight

Puritan leader Oliver Cromwell led the Roundhead army to victory over the Royalists in 1646, putting an end to the first English civil war.

among themselves instead of pursuing and capturing him. Instead of finding a safe haven, Charles was imprisoned by the Scots, who were still angry about his earlier attempt to impose Anglican rules on Presbyterians. But he was correct in predicting that the Roundheads would fight among themselves. A whole complex of disagreements surfaced in the two years after the war as groups tried to negotiate favorable power alliances. Soldiers demanded back pay. Supporters revolted and changed allegiance. Scots, who had fought with Parliament soldiers, now fought against them over religious freedom. Parliament's Puritans and independents disagreed over the attempt to restore Charles as king. The Scottish, the king's, and Parliament's armies were at odds. Cromwell, in charge of the Puritan army, grew impatient at the failure to reach a negotiated settlement. He took soldiers and went north to regain territory and settle disputes in a second civil war. Having had enough of bloodshed and enough suffering by families divided over the issues, the armies quit fighting in mid-1647. Meanwhile, Charles escaped to safety on the Isle of Wight off the southern coast of England.

Accused of Treason

When the fighting stopped, no one had authority to run the country, a situation that created an opportunity for a military takeover. When Parliament tried to restore Charles with limited power, Parliament's army leaders worried that a restored king might punish them for fighting against him. They controlled Parliament by permitting only the Puritan faithful to enter. On December 6, 1648, army leaders and troops barred entrance to Royalist and Presbyterian members, those they thought likely to be unfaithful to them. Of the five hundred members in the House of Commons in 1648, army leaders found only fifty-six members they felt were reliable. Those who remained after the army's purge were called the Rump Parliament. A Cromwell aide drew up a document demanding that the king be brought to justice and that the nation be made a republic. With a majority of six votes, this Parliament passed an ordinance that declared the king guilty of treason and on January 6 appointed a commission to try him. The members of the House of Lords objected. Hoping to avoid regicide, the killing of a king, the army leader offered another set of conditions to limit Charles's power and to protect the army. But Charles rejected this and all other conditional offers. When questioned about this Parliament's authority to try the king, Cromwell, according to historian Hugh Ross Williamson, lost his temper and said they would cut off the king's head with the crown on it.

Feelings about the severity of the king's guilt and the need to execute him were by no means unanimous. Centuries of tradition had taught the English people to regard their monarch with respect, and since the days of Elizabeth, Anglicans had sworn to accept the monarch's authority without question. The quick pace at which the king came to trial brought disquiet to the citizens, many leaders, and even the army. According to historian Williamson, the execution "was, indeed Cromwell's affair. . . . The High Court [commission appointed to try the king] was an expression of his individual will and purpose." Cromwell was angry because Charles had attempted from time to time to ally himself with the Scots, who were Presbyterians. Cromwell disliked Scottish Presbyterians only slightly less that he disliked Catholics. Worse yet, at one point Charles had tried to call in a Scottish army; to Cromwell, Scots were foreigners and calling them was "'Treason' . . . its intention . . . 'to vassalize [make dependent] us to a *foreign* nation.' "[11]

The Trial and Execution of Charles I

The procedures used in Charles's trial caused many citizens and leaders to doubt the wisdom of this action, but the government had no judicial system either to slow it down or to give the case against Charles a full hearing. Consequently, the trial went forward according to the ordinance passed by the Rump Parliament. The trial opened on January 20, 1649, in Westminster Hall. The appointed commissioners met in private to avoid risking a chance that public sympathy might turn to Charles. After three days, they met to sentence the king, but Cromwell had trouble getting enough signatures for the death warrant, though he eventually succeeded. Charles was brought before this court to hear the accusations against him. When told that he was accused of high treason and other crimes, he was asked to confess or deny. He refused to acknowledge that Parliament was a court and was taken away with his request for a hearing unrecognized. The day for sentencing was set for January 27. When the clerk read the sentence, he asked if Charles had any-

After declaring Charles guilty of high treason, Parliament brought him to trial.

thing to say in his defense; Charles again asked to be heard before both houses of Parliament. The clerk ignored Charles's request and listed the specific offenses and concluded, "for all which treasons and crimes this Court doth adjudge that the said Charles Stuart, as a tyrant, traitor, murderer and public enemy to the good people of this nation, shall be put to death by severing of his head from his body."[12] A public execution was set for January 30 on a scaffold outside the window of the second-story banqueting hall of Whitehall Palace, the king's residence. So that he could not hear the carpenters as they built his scaffold, he was moved from Whitehall to Saint James's Palace to await the final day.

The courage that Charles displayed at the trial and his behavior in the face of execution caused further doubt among leaders and elicited respect and sympathy from them and from citizens. At Saint James's Palace, Charles saw his youngest children and told Elizabeth, thirteen, not to grieve and Henry, ten, not to become a king. Having been a religious person all his life, Charles spent much of his remaining time with Bishop William Juxon, who read the Bible and prayed. Charles also talked with the two guards Cromwell had appointed, Matthew Tomlinson and Thomas Herbert, who had become his friends. Historian Hugh Ross Williamson reports:

On this last evening of his life, Charles turned to Tomlinson for friendship and advice. He called him into his room and discussed the speech he intended to make on the scaffold. . . . To this grave, courteous young man who, five weeks ago was unknown to him even by name, Charles, who had so little left to give, bequeathed his gold tooth-pick which he always carried in a case in his pocket. . . . [Then] the King made one last request. Would Tomlinson stay with him to the end? Tomlinson promised. Then he withdrew, leaving Charles alone with Herbert.[13]

At his trial Charles is declared "a tyrant, traitor, murderer, and public enemy" and sentenced to death.

The Execution of Charles I

Charles I went to his death with remarkable cooperation. In his book The Day They Killed the King, *historian Hugh Ross Williamson describes the moment of the ax blow and the crowd's reaction.*

"For a minute or two he stood in profound [deep] meditation. Then he murmured to himself a few inaudible words before he lay down with his head over the block and could no longer be seen by the spectators in the street. They saw nothing but the flash of the upraised axe before it crashed down and killed the King at its first falling.

Young Philip Henry in the crowd left it on record: 'At the instant when the blow was given there was such a dismal universal groan amongst the thousands of people who were in sight of it as it were with one consent, as I never heard before and desire I may never hear again.'"

Charles receives a final comforting word from a clergyman before ascending the scaffold to his death.

Charles explained to Herbert how to dispense with his books and requested that Herbert stay in his room for the night. On the way to the scaffold, Charles gave Herbert his little silver watch.

On the scaffold the two executioners, William Hulet and Hugh Peters, disguised in wigs and false beards, waited for the king. Midway in his prepared speech, Charles stopped when he saw one of the officials check the sharpness of the ax blade. Historian Williamson explains:

Charles was afraid that the edge would be blunted and so give him needless pain. He could not forget how his grandmother, Mary, Queen of Scots, had been hacked to death by blow after blow on the scaffold at Fotheringhay. "Hurt not the axe," he said, "that it may not hurt me."[14]

Then he finished his speech. After another reminder to take care with the ax, he gave his cloak, ring, and prayer book to Bishop Juxon. Charles took the white cap and tucked in his own hair so that his neck was bare, and he asked for a higher block on which to rest his head when they chopped it off. Charles looked out at the crowd and then said to the executioner: "I shall say but a short prayer and, when I hold out my hands thus, strike."[15] With one blow, the executioner severed his head. The assistant picked it up, showed it to the crowd, and slammed it down hard enough to bruise one cheek.

As soon as the body was removed, souvenir hunters bought bloodstained sand and wood and dipped handkerchiefs in the king's blood for a fee. Soldiers, who got the money, also sold Charles's hair. One was overheard to say, "I would we had two or three more Majestys to behead, if we could but make such use of them."[16] After lying in state, King Charles was buried at Windsor Castle near Oxford. English opinion about the execution was mixed: some people were glad to be rid of the king, others were indifferent, and some were sickened that it had taken place at all. Many people who were ruled by kings on the continent were shocked by Charles's execution.

In the confusion following the overthrow of the government and the execution of the king, Cromwell kept order in London and stood ready to put down revolts in Ireland and Scotland, countries that had been under the sovereignty of the English king. The Rump Parliament, the army, and Cromwell constructed a new government. The remaining fifty-six members in the House of Commons abolished the House of Lords and declared a king unnecessary. In May 1649 Parliament made Cromwell England's leader and proclaimed the nation a commonwealth, a state ruled by the people. He was to rule with the Council of State, a body of thirty-nine men, all nominated from the body of independent or Puritan candidates. When leaders of the commonwealth excluded Catholics and Anglicans from government and executed and imprisoned suspected Royalists, citizens responded with sympathy for those punished and began to think of Charles as a martyr. Since Parliament had been purged, many counties now had no representation in government. England had become less democratic than it had been under the Stuarts. Power essentially resided with the army, since only the army could maintain order and keep the Royalist rebels in England, Catholic rebels in Ireland, and Presbyterian rebels in Scotland from causing trouble. Trouble also arose from the Levelers, a group that wanted representation for the lower classes, and the Diggers, a group that wanted more land for the poor.

Cromwell's Power Grows

Cromwell first put down the Levelers and then took his army to Ireland, where he won battles through bloody cruelty. He confiscated Irish land and property, outlawed the Catholic religion, and sent selected Irish children to England for a Protestant education. Historian Maurice Ashley describes the effect of Cromwell's actions:

> Thus Cromwell's name came to be associated in Irish minds with starvation as well as slaughter and no later concessions made by English governments in the way of free trade or representation at Westminster could ever wipe away the awful curse from the memories of Irishmen. . . . Nothing could smooth away, hide, or bury the bitterness of those years which has helped to shape Irish history ever since.[17]

After subduing the Irish, Cromwell put down the Scots, who were shocked by Charles's execution and had proclaimed his son the rightful king, Charles II, six weeks after the death of his father. The Scots raised an army for Charles II, but Cromwell returned from Ireland and fought the Scots in the third civil war.

When Cromwell defeated the Scots in 1652, he became the most powerful person in England.

Since England still had no constitution that designated the powers of government, Cromwell and Parliament spent most of the years in the 1650s trying to form a plan for making the commonwealth work. Parliament had proposed new elections to give representation to districts throughout the nation, adding 344 members to the 56 left in the Rump Parliament. Cromwell lost patience with the lengthy debate that resulted from the larger, more diverse Parliament and dismissed it. For a time he and the army ruled alone. Then they tried a Parliament with members nominated by the military. The military Parliament tried to create a new constitution, but that goal failed over disagreement on religious matters. Finally, army leaders proposed a set of rules called

To keep the Scots from bringing Charles II to the throne, Cromwell and his troops suppress the Presbyterian rebels in Scotland.

the Instrument of Government. This document appointed Cromwell to a lifetime position called Lord Protector of the Commonwealth of England, Scotland, and Ireland, a position with many of the same powers the king once had. This document also set up a second chamber in Parliament, a replacement for the dismissed House of Lords, to advise Cromwell and the regularly elected Parliament. In 1653 Cromwell signed the Instrument of Government, the closest thing to a written constitution England has ever had, before or after the civil wars.

Since no system of checks and balances existed, the sessions of Parliament degenerated into a chaos of disagreements. For two years Cromwell called and

Ireland's Prosperity Out of Cromwell's Cruelty

Oliver Cromwell's brutal war against the Irish brought discipline and prosperity for a time. In volume one of his book The History of England, *Thomas Babington Macaulay gives his nineteenth-century version of Cromwell's action and the results that followed.*

"But everything yielded to the vigour and ability of Cromwell. In a few months he subjugated Ireland, as Ireland had never been subjugated during the five centuries of slaughter which had elapsed since the landing of the first Norman settlers. He resolved to put an end to that conflict of races and religions which had so long distracted the island, by making the English and Protestant population decidedly predominant. For this end he gave the rein to the fierce enthusiasm of his followers, waged war resembling that which Israel waged on the Canaanites, smote the idolaters [idol worshipers] with the edge of the sword, so that great cities were left without inhabitants, drove many thousands to the Continent, shipped off many thousands to the West Indies, and supplied the void thus made by pouring in numerous colonists, of Saxon [English] blood, and of Calvinistic [Protestant] faith. Strange to say, under that iron rule, the conquered country began to wear an outward face of prosperity. Districts, which had recently been as wild as those where the first settlers of Connecticut were contending with the red men, were in a few years transformed into the likeness of Kent and Norfolk [English counties]. New buildings, roads, and plantations were everywhere seen. The rent of estates rose fast; and soon the English landowners began to complain that they were met in every market by the products of Ireland, and to clamour for protecting laws."

Cromwell, shown dismissing Parliament, led a regime that suppressed the English people and failed to solve the nation's problems.

dismissed Parliament much as the Stuart kings had done. Finally, Cromwell established twelve military districts and governed them by martial law, using the army to keep order. England found itself a nation in which citizens were taxed without representation or parliamentary approval, arrested without due process of law, brought to trial without a jury, and governed by force of the army. With neither the tradition of a monarchy nor the constitutional mechanism of a representative government, the commonwealth had no guidelines. Cromwell, though an effective military leader, lacked the skills to bring vision, cooperation, compromise, and unity to the commonwealth. Cromwell's rule was hated as no government in England has been hated, before or since. There was talk of assassinating him. As objections mounted, Cromwell tightened his rule, using stricter censorship, spying, arrests, and punishment to protect it. Cromwell called his last Parliament in Jan-

uary 1658, but the two houses fought, and Cromwell dismissed them. In the fall of 1658, Cromwell died, and his son Richard took over. A spirit of rebellion spread, and the English people began to call for restoration of the monarchy and for Prince Charles to become king.

The Puritan Revolution

Besides causing great political changes, Puritan, or Roundhead, victory in the civil war brought a revolution in religion. After the breakup of Anglicanism, religion was free from state control for a time until 1654. Then Cromwell appointed a Puritan commission to establish rules for religion and to test clergymen for their fitness to receive stipends, or salaries, which were traditionally paid by Parliament. The commission declared that only Puritans, Baptists, and Presbyterians were eligible for stipends. By 1657 it had established rules that resulted in persecution of Catholics, Anglicans, and other Protestant dissenters. For example, one man was arrested for attending a secret Anglican service, and two Catholic priests were hanged. A 1657 law required all landowners over sixteen to disavow Catholicism or forfeit two-thirds of their property. A Quaker named James Nayler was arrested for blasphemy, or speaking against the established religion. After debating his case for eleven days, Parliament voted not to execute, but to give him a more humane punishment, which was two hours with his neck in a pillory, 310 lashes, the letter B burned into his forehead, a hole bored through his

Under Cromwell's brutal rule, non-Puritans such as Quaker James Nayler were accused of blasphemy and tortured.

tongue with a red-hot iron, an imprisonment in solitary confinement, without pen, paper, fire, or light. In short, the Puritans, who had objected to Charles's absolute rule, now ruled with a similar authority and cruelty.

Puritan Beliefs

In addition, by 1657 Oliver Cromwell and his Puritan colleagues had passed regulations to impose their moral and social order on English society. Puritan speech was serious and slow, filled with biblical phrases and imagery. Their clothes were somber and plain. Puritans suspected that beautiful women lacked virtue, but female plainness, motherhood, and faithfulness met their approval. Puritans fostered Bible reading and frowned on entertainment. They closed all theaters between 1642 and 1656 and prohibited horse races, cockfights, wrestling matches, and bear and bull baiting, the sport of setting dogs on a chained animal. They disapproved of all music except hymns and all art except portraits. They designated Wednesday as a day of fasting, and Sunday as a day of strict religious observation: no shops open, no games or sports, no business transacted, no unavoidable travel, and no walking for pleasure. Anglican control had been mild by comparison. People who were not Puritans had little reason to comply with the rules. As a result, citizens became hypocrites; they complied with the Puritan rules in public, but they acted otherwise in private. One historian suggests that the rules may have strengthened the will and character of the people, but their rigidity also narrowed the people's minds.

Oliver Cromwell's Convictions

Historians seem to agree that Oliver Cromwell was often a brutal and authoritarian ruler, but Maurice Ashley portrays another side of Cromwell's personality in his book England in the Seventeenth Century.

"Cromwell in his heart believed in what most people mean by freedom, the freedom of the mind, the freedom of the spirit. He maintained that it was 'an unjust and unwise jealousy to deprive a man of his natural liberty upon a supposition that he may abuse it: when he doth abuse it', he added, then 'judge'. Cromwell believed that the mind was the man. He thought all Christians had a right within limits to seek truth in their own fashion. He said in an immortal phrase: 'To be a Seeker is to be of the best sect after a Finder, and such a one shall every faithful humble Seeker be in the end.' It is true that Cromwell's idea of 'liberty of conscience' was narrow by modern standards. It did not, for instance, apply to Roman Catholics or even to the Anglicans. But it embraced both the Quakers and the Jews so long as they did not defy civil authority. Those political and economic freedoms which came down to us with the spirit of nonconformity we owe in no small measure to the precepts [principles] of Oliver Cromwell."

Soon after Oliver Cromwell's son had become lord protector, Parliament and the army with all its divisions overthrew him. Richard Cromwell resigned on May 25, 1659, and disappeared into France. England had no leader, and the English feared anarchy, that is, political disorder and confusion. No remaining force or group was strong enough to oppose the military rule. Only another army could wrench power from Parliament's army. A general favorable to the monarchy, George Monck, had ten thousand soldiers in Scotland to maintain order there. On December 5, 1659, he led those forces into England, and the Parliament army did not fight. Monck and his forces reached London on February 3, 1660, and called for a new, freely elected Parliament, an act which meant that Prince Charles would be installed as King Charles II. Monck sent Sir John Greenville to give Charles the message to come to England to be the king. The civil war and the interregnum, or period without a king, were over. In light of Cromwell and the Puritan commonwealth, the people felt that a monarchy with its faults seemed better.

Chapter

3 From Restoration to Disarray, 1660–1685

In 1660 many English people and their leaders felt both relieved and optimistic—relieved that they had averted Puritan domination, rule by the military, and anarchy, and optimistic that the restoration of a monarchy would return their nation to the order and stability of the past. With great enthusiasm the nation heard the news that Prince Charles had agreed to return as king. On May 8, 1660, Prince Charles was proclaimed Charles II, King of England, a title backdated to the moment of his father's death, thereby making the monarchy continuous.

King Charles II arrived in the port city of Dover on May 25, 1660, welcomed by an excited crowd of twenty thousand gathered on the beach. Samuel Pepys, writer and public servant of the time, recorded in his diary:

> Infinite the crowd of people and the horsemen, citizens, and noblemen of all sorts. The Mayor of the town came and gave him his white staff, the badge of his place, which the King did give him again. The Mayor also presented him from the town a very rich Bible, which he took and said it was the thing that he loved above all things in the world. A canopy was provided for him to stand under, which he did, and

talked awhile with General Monk [Monck] and others, and so into a stately coach there set for him, and so away through the town towards Canterbury, without making any stay at Dover. The shouting and joy expressed by all is past imagination.[18]

Charles II was welcomed as king of England by many who feared Puritan domination and hoped that the return of the monarchy would restore the order of the past.

The Coronation of Charles II

For centuries monarchs in England have been crowned in Westminster Abbey. Writer Samuel Pepys recorded his impression of the coronation of Charles II in his Diary. *This excerpt is quoted by Bernard D. Grebanier et al. in their book,* English Literature and Its Backgrounds.

"April 23, 1661. About 4 I rose and got to the Abbey, . . . where with a great deal of patience I sat from past 4 till 11 before the King came in. And a great pleasure it was to see the Abbey raised in the middle, all covered with red, and a throne (that is a chair) and a footstool on the top of it; and all the officers of all kinds, so much as the very fiddlers, in red vests. At last comes in the Dean and Prebends [members of the clergy] of Westminster, with the Bishops (many of them in cloth of gold copes [long vestments]), and after them the Nobility, all in their Parliament robes, which was a most magnificent sight. Then the Duke, and the King. . . . The King in his robes, bareheaded, which was very fine. And after all had placed themselves, there was a sermon, and the service; . . . the King passed through all the ceremonies of the Coronation. . . . The crown being put upon his head, a great shout begun, and he came forth to the throne, and there passed more ceremonies: as taking the oath, and having things read to him by the Bishop."

Four days later when King Charles II arrived in London, 120,000 of the city's inhabitants greeted him. Historians Ariel and Will Durant describe the reception as

such popular rejoicing as exceeded anything in England's memory. Twenty thousand men of the city militia escorted him, flaunting their banners and brandishing their swords, through streets strewn with flowers, hung with tapestry, noisy with trumpets and bells and hailing cries. . . . It marked the temper of England, and the failure of Puritanism.[19]

Before Parliament held coronation ceremonies, however, members met with Charles to clarify the distribution of power between the king and Parliament.

Conscious of the civil wars and the execution of a king in the recent past, both Charles II and Parliament proceeded carefully to clarify their roles. The Restoration Settlement defined the roles of Parliament, the king, and the church. It restored Parliament to the role it had before the Puritan-dominated Parliament changed it: it restored the system of electing representatives, restored the House of Lords, and reinstated bishops as members of the

Excited crowds greet their new king as Charles begins a procession through the streets of London.

House of Lords. In addition, the Settlement redefined the role of the king. The king could no longer use prerogative courts to arrest and punish his enemies. He could no longer levy taxes not approved by Parliament or make laws by royal prerogative. Yet, the king could still veto laws, command the militia, and exercise power except in matters of money. Finally, the Settlement restored the Church of England with all its bishops and deans. Thus, Parliament and the king now shared power equally.

Charles II's Personality

Besides the joy of having their church and state restored, most of the English people were happy with their new king. A letter supposedly written by a Londoner named Samuel Tuke on May 6, 1660, describes Charles:

He is somewhat taller then the middle stature of *English men*; so exactly form'd, that the most curious eye cannot finde one error in his shape. His face is rather grave then severe, which is very much softened whensoever he speaks; His complexion is somewhat dark, but much enlightened by his eyes, which are quick and sparkling. . . . His haire, which he hath in great plenty, is of a shining black, not frizled, but so naturally curling into great rings, that it is a very comely ornament.[20]

Charles had a learned mind, a charming wit, and a generous nature to enhance his attractive appearance. He had a liberal education and excelled in navigation and sailing. With manners polished during his years in France, he had learned tolerance for others' opinions and easily drank toasts to the health of his opponents. He enjoyed humor, told stories with a flair, and engaged in quick satire and jokes even about himself. His good nature extended to generosity. He gave to charities and built a park as a sanctuary for animals. Historian Thomas Babington

Macaulay, however, viewed his generosity with skepticism:

> Worthless men and women, to the very bottom of whose hearts he saw, . . . could easily wheedle him out of titles, places, domains, state secrets and pardons. He bestowed much. . . . The consequence was that his bounty generally went, not to those who deserved it best, nor even to those whom he liked best, but to the most shameless and importunate [overly persistent] suitor who could obtain an audience.[21]

Nonetheless, for many of the English people, Charles's initial good impression lasted throughout his reign. Charles told his subjects that he wanted to be a king who pleased his subjects with his generosity, friendliness, and style. Historian Godfrey Davies explains: "When he died, we are told, Londoners were as sorrowful as if they all belonged to one family that had lost a common parent. . . . As a person he was popular beyond a doubt. He had probably the most captivating manners of any English sovereign."[22]

The Clarendon Code

The euphoria accompanying the king's return soon gave way to reality, and old antagonisms resurfaced. Now in the majority, Anglican members in Parliament were determined to keep Puritans from obtaining power again. Anglicans and Royalists had had enough of the Puritans' restrictive moral laws. Between 1662 and 1665, Parliament passed a series of six acts to secure the authority of the Church of England. These acts, called the Clarendon Code, were named for the earl of Clarendon. The Corporation Act required all officeholders in state and municipal government to take religious sacrament according to the rites of the Church of England and to swear allegiance to the king. Another decree required that a revised version of the *Book of Common Prayer* be used in all worship services. The Act of Uniformity stated that all clergy who did not agree to use the revised *Book of Common Prayer* must forfeit their living stipends. The Licensing Act gave the bishop of London and the archbishop of Canterbury, both Anglican officials, large powers over the press. Parliament replaced the Uniformity Act with another act that punished people for attending services not conducted according to the *Book of Common Prayer*. Finally, the Five Mile Act banned Nonconformist preachers from living in or visiting any place where they formerly had been ministers. Nonconformists, who also became known as Dissenters, were those unwilling to conform to the Church of England.

The Clarendon Code had punitive results for Nonconformists. By August 1662 many clergy—between one thousand and two thousand—had been driven from parishes for dissenting, and many were later imprisoned. For example, the famous writer John Bunyan, who had joined the Baptist Church, was imprisoned for preaching in the streets. Charles, who was supposed to enforce the Clarendon Code, only halfheartedly cooperated with his Royalist supporters in doing so. He would have preferred to use his royal prerogative to give relief to both Catholics and Protestant dissenters. In a paper called the Declaration of Indulgence, he explained how he wanted to soften the severity of the code. The House of Commons, however, forced Charles to withdraw his paper. From then on, Charles enforced the Clarendon Code only because he had to convince Parliament to grant him money.

The personal charm of Charles II belied many of the king's real motives and faults, among them his inclination to indulge in lavish pleasures. Among those who were particularly aware, Charles developed the reputation as a ruler who "never said a foolish thing or did a wise one," according to historians T. Walter Wallbank and Alastair M. Taylor.[23] Charles dedicated little of his time to work and governing and much of his time to pleasures. Historian Thomas Babington Macaulay describes Charles's laziness:

> He was utterly without ambition. He detested business, and would sooner have abdicated [given up] his crown than have undergone the trouble of really directing the administration. Such was his aversion to toil, and such his ignorance of affairs, that the very clerks who attended him when he sate [sat] in council could not refrain from sneering at his frivolous remarks, and at his childish impatience.[24]

Macaulay says that Charles was "addicted beyond measure to sensual indulgence, fond of sauntering and frivolous amusements, [and] incapable of self-denial."[25] He had thirteen known mistresses and eight illegitimate sons. Charles also indulged in dancing, horse races, cockfights, gambling, and drinking. In 1662 he married Catherine of Braganza, daughter of John IV, king of Portugal, and told her that adultery was a royal privilege. One of his mistresses was Nell Gwynn, a London actress of questionable reputation. He had another mistress sent from France. Ariel and Will Durant report that

More interested in frivolous amusements than the administration of the country, Charles indulges in a grand feast at his palace.

once when Nell was riding in a coach, people on the street mistook her for the French Catholic mistress and jeered at her. Nell "put her pretty head out of the coach window and cried, 'Be silent, good people; I am the *Protestant* whore.'"[26]

Though Charles was perhaps the most scandalous ruler of his time, he remained popular, perhaps because he reflected society's manners and morals. After years of Puritan restrictive laws and moral restraints, the end of Puritan control let loose a wave of high fashion and low morals. Men of the court and gentry wore wigs, velvet breeches, or pants, and coats decorated with ribbons and lace. Women powdered and perfumed their hair, pasted beauty spots on their faces, and wore dresses cut to reveal shoulders and breasts. The rich indulged in lavish feasts and drank imported wine. Free again, they played lawn bowling, cricket, billiards, cards, and floor games. They scorned virtue and marital fidelity; the higher the rank, the lower the morals. Unfaithful wives were as common as unfaithful husbands. Though the lower classes and commoners had less means to be wicked, they too enjoyed the new freedom to attend puppet shows, circuses, and wrestling matches.

Economic Issues

Beneath the surface of frivolity and pleasure lay the reality of economic changes and problems that prevented a return to the stable past. Though the House of Commons accommodated the king's need for money by taxing beer, ale, coffee, and tea, the king was still short of money. Be-

Charles considered adultery a royal privilege. Here, he woos one of his mistresses, Nell Gwynn.

sides inheriting a huge debt of three million pounds and a bill for Royalist soldiers' back pay, Charles II, like his grandfather, James I, wanted money to finance his entertainment and his expensive style of living.

New developments in the English economy again created changes among the social classes and further compounded the king's economic problems. Between 1660 and 1688 English commercial ventures doubled and became more important than land ownership, the traditional source of wealth for the aristocracy. Entrepreneurs and merchants developed colonies in New York, New Jersey, Pennsylvania, Carolina,

Canada, and East Africa. They developed companies like the East India Company and gained rights to trade for huge profits in India. As a result, the gentry and middle classes grew both in numbers and wealth. Hundreds of London gentry owned gold and set up banks, which paid 6 percent on deposits and charged 8 percent on loans. To avoid letting Parliament control his allowance, Charles, still in debt, borrowed from these bankers. Historian Maurice Ashley sums up the significant economic changes: "Changes in methods of public finance, as well as changes in the ownership of landed property, strengthened the power of the wealthy English magnates [businessmen] at the expense of the Crown and ushered in a new era of history."[27]

London's Plague and Fire

To dampen the euphoria further, London experienced two accidents, a plague in 1665 followed by a major fire in 1666. Brought in on ships from foreign ports, infected black rats carried their fleas around the city and spread the bubonic plague. A highly contagious and usually fatal disease, it spread quickly, especially among the poor, who lived in crowded conditions. Once bitten by the fleas, people developed chills, fever, vomiting, and swollen bumps. One historian estimated that sixty-eight thousand died in London.

Londoners were just recovering from the plague when a fire started in Pudding Lane on September 2, 1666. After a long drought, old wood and plaster houses built close together ignited easily, and fire spread quickly in a strong wind. By the

Victims of the bubonic plague that devastated London in 1665 are taken off the street and loaded onto a cart.

time it was put out on September 7, the fire had destroyed a one-by-two-mile area in the heart of London, having burned 13,200 houses, 89 churches, and most bookstalls along the Thames River. Out of the wreckage, though, London organized a fire department, improved sanitation, built with brick rather than wood, and made wider, straighter streets. The most significant benefit after the fire was the

The Great Fire of London

Writer Samuel Pepys saw the London fire from several places in the city. Excerpts from his Diary, *as quoted by Bernard D. Grebanier et al., describe its destruction during the five days that the city burned.*

"September 2 (Lord's day), 1666. Jane [a maid] called us up about three in the morning, to tell us of a great fire they saw in the City. So I rose and . . . went to her window. . . . By and by Jane comes and tells me that she hears that above 300 houses have been burned down tonight by the fire we saw, and that it was now burning down all Fish-street, by London Bridge. So I . . . walked to the Tower. . . . So down, with my heart full of trouble, to the Lieutenant of the Tower, who tells me that it begun this morning in the King's baker's house in Pudding-lane, and that it hath burned St. Magnus's Church and most part of Fish-street already. . . . Everybody endeavoring to remove their goods, and flinging into the river or bringing them into lighters [barges] that lay off [shore]; poor people staying in their houses as long as till the very fire touched them, and then running into boats, or clambering from one pair of stairs by the waterside to another. And among other things, the poor pigeons, I perceive, were loth [loath] to leave their houses, but hovered about the windows and balconys till they were, some of them burned, their wings, and fell down. . . . As it grew darker, [the fire] appeared more and more, and in corners and upon steeples, and between churches and houses, as far as we could see up the hill of the City, in a most horrid malicious bloody flame, not like the fine flame of an ordinary fire.

September 4, 1666. Up at break of day to get away the remainder of my things . . . and saw how horridly the sky looks, all on a fire in the night, was enough to put us out of our wits; and, indeed, it was extremely dreadful, for it looks just as if it was at us, and the whole heaven on fire."

work of the famous architect Christopher Wren, who used his talents in the rebuilding of Saint Paul's Cathedral.

Though the upper classes had enough wealth to rebuild the city after the fire, the king still had debts and an allowance inadequate for his expenses. To obtain money, he made secret alliances with Louis XIV of France between 1670 and 1681. The first was the Treaty of Dover. France gave Charles a sum of money; in return, Charles agreed to restore Catholicism in England and to support Louis XIV in a war with Holland. Then Charles turned and persuaded Parliament to raise money for a war against the French king. France was Charles's secret ally and Parliament's enemy. Historians Wallbank and Taylor called the Treaty of Dover "one of the most scandalous actions ever committed by an English king, . . . [a] performance of running with the hare and hunting with the hounds and making everybody like it."[28] In other words, Charles was playing two opposite sides at the same time, trying to benefit from both. In the other four secret treaties with France, Charles received more money; in return, he agreed to dissolve Parliament should Parliament want war with France.

The Test Act

Two years after the first treaty, Charles began his plan to restore Catholicism. In 1672 he precipitated a political crisis when he used his divine right to suspend Parliament's laws against Catholics. Suspicious of Charles's motives, Parliament countered by passing the Test Act in 1673. This act made it illegal for a person to hold any office in the government or in the military without having taken the sacrament according to the rules of the Anglican Church. In other words, the Test Act expanded the Corporation Act in the Clarendon Code. Its purpose was to ex-clude Catholics from all public offices; its framers also wanted to make sure that it prevented Charles's brother James, already a Catholic, from succeeding to the throne. The Test Act kept Catholics, and some Protestant Nonconformists, out of public office for 150 years until it was repealed in 1829.

Because members in Parliament had a growing suspicion about the king's intentions concerning Catholics, they took special precautions. Members from the House of Commons gathered at a local tavern to discuss ways to stop Charles from succeeding in his goal to make England Catholic again. They called themselves the Green Ribbon Club and took as their motto, "life, liberty, and property." In response, Anglicans and members of the landed aristocracy formed a group and took as their motto, "the king, the church, and the land." From this beginning, the members of the Green Ribbon Club developed into the Whig Party, and the landed wealthy developed into the Tory Party. Both parties formed strategies for persuading voters and winning elections.

Remembering that the father of Charles II had used his royal prerogative to imprison his enemies in the Tower of London and often had them executed without trial, Parliament wanted to head off any similar actions that Charles II might take. To protect leaders who spoke in opposition to the king, Parliament passed the Habeas Corpus Act. This act said that any person who thought he or she had been imprisoned unjustly could obtain a writ of habeas corpus; the writ compelled the government to explain why the individual had lost his or her liberty. It provided citizens a safeguard against illegal imprisonment without a judicial hearing.

False Plots Against the King

Parliament remained suspicious of Charles's intentions, and Charles kept his goal a secret by manipulating people and situations. No public crisis occurred even though suspicions increased and tensions mounted until August 28, 1678, when a citizen named Titus Oates appeared before the king and announced that he had learned of a popish, or Catholic, plot. The son of an Anabaptist preacher, Titus Oates had become an Anglican clergyman, but he was expelled from his post for disorderly conduct. Then he supposedly converted to Catholicism and studied in a

Titus Oates revealed a plot to kill Charles and replace him with the Catholic James.

Catholic college, from which he was also expelled. According to Oates, the pope, the king of France, the archbishop of Armagh in northern Ireland, and Jesuit priests from England, Ireland, and Spain were planning to kill Charles and put the Catholic James on the throne. They were planning to impose Catholicism by sword. Three hundred cutthroats were to arrive and massacre Protestants and burn London, the home of English Protestantism, to the ground.

At first the king and Parliament laughed at Oates's story as a preposterous hoax. Shortly after, however, a letter and a mysterious murder provided enough evidence to make the plot plausible in the minds of those already tense and suspicious. Parliament acted quickly by impeaching, or removing from office, five Catholic members of the House of Lords and committing them to the Tower of London. In addition, Parliament passed a bill excluding Catholics from both Commons and Lords. In January, Charles dissolved this Cavalier, or Royalist, Parliament, which he feared might pass an exclusion bill that would prohibit his brother from becoming the next king. In March the first Whig Parliament was elected, a more anti-Catholic and anti-king Parliament than the previous one. This Parliament proposed a bill to prevent James from ever ascending the throne, and Charles offered to compromise in order to save his brother's chances.

Since England still had no democratic institutions to designate the procedures to follow in solving crises and no independent justice department to protect citizens, order broke down again as it had in earlier decades. The next year, 1679, brought accusations and executions, wild tales of other plots, and intensified hatred of

Catholics. Catholics whom Oates accused were quickly tried, found guilty, and executed. The Act of Habeas Corpus mattered little because the bloodthirsty crowds calling for punishment outside the court frightened judges from taking action. Seeing the effect of Oates's accusations, others came forth with ever wilder tales. Historian Thomas Babington Macaulay explains:

> A wretch named Carstairs . . . led the way. Bedloe, noted swindler, followed; and soon from all the brothels, gambling houses, and spunging houses [places of confinement for debtors] of London, false witnesses poured forth to swear away the lives of Roman Catholics. One came with a story about an army of thirty thousand men who were to muster in the disguise of pilgrims at Corunna [in Spain], and to sail thence to Wales. Another had been promised canonisation [sainthood] and five hundred pounds to murder the King. . . . Oates . . . soon added a large supplement to his original narrative, . . . that he had once stood behind a door which was ajar, and had there overheard the Queen declare that she had resolved to give her consent to the assassination of her husband. The vulgar [uneducated] believed, and the highest magistrates pretended to believe, even such fictions as these.[29]

Anti-Catholic arrests and executions occurred until Oates made a mistake in his testimony against the queen's doctor. Once Londoners realized that there was no real plot, the intense fear and hate subsided. Thinking people, however, realized that Oates and his lies had sent many innocent people to early deaths.

The Exclusion Issue

Between 1679 and 1681 Charles and the Whig Parliament quarreled bitterly over the issue of exclusion of Catholics, and antagonisms turned to hostilities. Amid all of these crises, Charles changed: he abandoned his playboy life and dedicated himself to politics and to the administration of the country. The more Charles favored Catholics, the more the Whig Parliament opposed Charles and tried to exclude James from the throne. The more the Whigs opposed Charles and James, the more the Tories favored them. The conflicts between the king and the Whigs and between the Whigs and the Tories began to resemble the situation in 1640 before the civil war. By this time both Whigs and Tories were effective political campaigners. When local county elections took on the national issue of who should succeed Charles, the two parties launched intense campaigns. The Whigs wanted the duke of Monmouth, Charles's illegitimate son, and the Tories wanted James, Charles's brother. The political fights were bitter, and many thought another civil war was inevitable. When mobs made London dangerous, Parliament moved to Oxford.

The Whigs lost power in the early 1680 elections. They had been so strong in their opposition to the king that a backlash of sympathy for the king set in, and many Whigs were persecuted. In 1683 in this atmosphere of anger, two Whig extremists reported another plot to assassinate the king near Rye House in Hertfordshire when the king was on his way to the horse races at Newmarket. Like the Oates plot, this one was also made up. Whig leaders and soldiers were arrested, and Tories enacted their revenge by throwing Whigs out of local offices, out of the army, and off judicial benches. Many were executed, and some fled to exile in Holland. After the Whig defeat, Charles asserted his power by dissolving the Oxford Parliament and ruling without one.

The Death of Charles II

On February 2, 1685, with no warning, Charles II suffered a convulsion: his face distorted and his mouth foamed. His doctor tried many remedies to cure Charles. He bled him, put cupping glasses to his shoulder to bring blood to the surface of his skin, cut his hair to raise blisters on his scalp, applied a plaster of pitch and pigeon dung to the soles of his feet, blew hellebore (a toxic plant) up his nostrils to remove fluids from his brain, poured antimony (a metallic element used today in battery plates) and sulfate of zinc down his throat to make him vomit, and gave him strong laxatives. None of the remedies improved the king's health. On February 4 he received the last rites of the Anglican Church, but Charles wanted a Catholic priest. With the priest, Charles professed his Catholic faith, confessed his sins, pardoned his enemies, and received the sacrament of extreme unction, or last rites. After asking his wife's pardon, he asked James to take care of his children and his French mistress. Among his last words, he said, "And do not let poor Nelly

At the end of Charles's reign the government of England was left in a state of chaos.

starve." At noon on February 6, 1685, Charles II died, and his brother became King James II. Charles had returned to London to a cheering and excited city and had remained popular with ordinary Londoners, but his deception had raised suspicions in Parliament, and his determination to return England to Catholicism had put the government in disarray.

Chapter

4 From Absolutism to Rebellion, 1685–1688

After three Stuart reigns a pattern had emerged in the relationship between the kings and Parliament, starting with mild conflict in the reign of James I and accelerating thereafter. Each Stuart king began by promising to uphold the laws of the state and its Anglican Church, but soon after, each acted, in greater or lesser degree, in favor of Dissenters and, especially, Catholics. Conflicts arose over money, individuals lost rights, and violence followed. At the end of each reign the government was in a state of discontent or disarray. The fourth Stuart king fell into the same pattern, but James II exceeded the level of conflict in a number of ways. Each government had tried to make a constitutional monarchy work, and none succeeded. A modern reader might well remember that no one in the seventeenth century—not the people, Parliament, or the king—had ever heard of a constitutional democracy with its checks and balances and its functional institutions because a constitutional democracy had yet to exist.

The fourth Stuart, James II, ascended the throne in 1685 when Charles II died. He followed the pattern of the other Stuarts in terms of promises, conflicts, and money. But he was also different from the other Stuart kings in important ways. He

was already a devout Catholic when he accepted the Crown. Moreover, he was less willing to compromise his divine right to rule than his predecessors, and as a result he was more willing to use violent means to attain power. And he was more determined to bring England under Catholic control.

The crowning of James II on February 6, 1685, relieved Anglican churchmen because it meant England had averted another civil war. James immediately took advantage of their enthusiasm. Speaking to the Privy Council, or advisory council, assembled to make his title official, James assured councilmen that he would preserve the church and state. As quoted by historian Godfrey Davies, he told the assembly:

> I shall make it my endeavours to preserve this government both in church and state as it is now by law establish'd: I know the principles of the Church of England are for monarchy, and the members of it have showed themselves good and loyal subjects, therefore I shall always take care to defend and support it: I know too, that the laws of England are sufficient to make the King as great a monarch as I can wish; and as I shall never depart from the

The coronation of James II brought to power a Catholic king after three Stuart reigns of Anglican kings. James appointed Anglicans to important posts, however, and gained the initial favor of his subjects.

just rights and prerogative of the crown, so I shall never invade any mans property; I have often heretofore ventured my life in defence of this nation, and I shall still go as far as any man in preserving it in all its just rights and liberties.[30]

His speech was published and its content spread to towns and villages, giving the people throughout the nation joy that their traditions would be secure. James further pleased the people by appointing Anglicans to important posts and by calling a Parliament. Thus, James II began his reign as a popular king.

The King's Pro-Catholic Actions

Soon, however, James openly associated with Catholics and began undoing anti-Catholic acts passed in the previous reign. The king, who had recently promised to defend and support the Church of England, openly attended daily Catholic mass and took some of his councilors with him. He released prisoners who had refused to take Anglican oaths of allegiance according to the Clarendon Code. He freed thousands of Catholics, twelve hundred Quakers, and many other Dissenters, but the action caused no alarm because the public was already sympathetic toward religious prisoners. In the winter of 1685 James asked Parliament to repeal the Test Act—the act that required a person to take sacrament according to Anglican rules in order to hold government or military office. He also asked Parliament to vote money for an army for his own purposes. Parliament refused both. Historian George Macaulay Trevelyan suggests that the Glorious Revolution really began when the Tories first opposed James and voted against these two requests. James had a choice—to compromise or to "drive straight on over all laws." James chose the second course. According to Trevelyan, James believed that his father, Charles I, "had fallen by making concessions: he would never, he declared, repeat that mistake."[31]

Rebellions Against James II

Within a year after he was crowned, fear was spreading that James intended to carry out Charles II's plan to make England Catholic. Two military actions developed to overthrow James before he could enact such a plan. A Scot, Archibald Campbell, earl of Argyll, led the first rebellion. Argyll landed the first week in May in the Western Isles of Scotland, was overcome on June 17, 1685, by James's army, and executed on June 30. James, Duke of Monmouth and son of Charles II, led the second rebellion. Equipped by Prince William of Orange, a Dutch state, Monmouth landed in southwestern England on June 11 and was there joined by a makeshift band of Puritans, some armed only with scythes, implements for cutting grain by hand. With no help from the moneyed classes, the invasions had no chance to succeed. James II sent his army against the forces led by Monmouth and defeated them on July 6, 1685. Monmouth fled and begged his uncle for forgiveness, but James had him beheaded. After the

Fear that James II was going to bring England under Catholic control led the duke of Monmouth (pictured) to attempt to overthrow the king.

defeat James gave orders that Monmouth's followers be tried. For the trial James set up the Court of High Commission with George Jeffreys as the chief justice. Jeffreys and his court found the rebels guilty and hanged four hundred men and sent eight hundred into forced labor in the West Indies. Because they were so brutal, these trials, or assizes, were called the Bloody Assizes. Historian Thomas Babington Macaulay comments: "Jeffreys had done his work, and returned to claim his reward. He arrived at Windsor from the West, leaving carnage, mourning, and terror behind him. The hatred with which he was regarded by the people . . . has no parallel in history. It was not quenched by time or by political changes."[32]

James II's Character

After the execution of Monmouth, "King James hardened his heart and went his way," says historian Maurice Ashley.[33] Historians call James "stubborn," "proud," "stupid," and "cynical." Historians have looked for clues to explain his hardheartedness. For much of his childhood and youth, James lived outside of his family and country. At nine he saw the civil war from Oxford and his father's defeat. After the war he was imprisoned, but he escaped, disguised as a girl, to live with his sister in Holland, where he was when his father, Charles I, was executed. His mother neglected him, and James grew up with little education or personal discipline. James had been an attractive child, but a long jaw and a narrow nose made him look arrogant and disagreeable as a

grown man. At eighteen he joined the French army and later the Spanish army, but he returned to England in 1660 when his brother Charles became king.

James was an ardent Catholic, converted to the faith in his midthirties. He believed that the only road to forgiveness and salvation was through his church. In his mind Catholics could be trusted; Protestants were rebels against God, and, therefore, their loyalty to him was suspect. Since he believed that God intervened or acted in earthly affairs—big or small, personal or national—he felt that God guided him when his affairs went well, but he became demoralized and depressed when affairs went badly. Historian J. R. Jones says: "The importance of James's conversion to Catholicism cannot be overstated. It was simple, sincere and irrevocable. His new faith made James certain that he was right, giving additional meaning and intensity to his belief in divine right principles."[34] This dedicated Catholic reigned in a country where his subjects hated Catholics and feared their takeover, a situation that affected the king's relationship with both Parliament and the nation.

James followed to the letter his father's theory of absolute authority, thus blinding him to any limitations of the monarchy. James was critical of his father, Charles I, and his brother, Charles II, for not standing firmly enough on the theory of absolutism. James relied on his authority and belief in his rightness. Maurice Ashley writes of him:

Always in the background of his mind was the menace to the English monarchy of another civil war and the wistful belief that only a toughness which neither his father nor his brother had ever shown could prevent the worst from happening. On the whole, he pictured the political landscape in black and white; those who were not with him were against him.[35]

Consequently, his personality and his outlook on the world left James a suspicious man who fell prey to flatterers. To maintain favor with the king and perhaps to save their lives, his ministers, or government officials, told James only what he wanted to hear. All ministers knew that power-hungry rivals watched and would take advantage of any mistake they might make or any sign of the king's disapproval. "So strong were [James's] prejudices, and so feeble his genius, that he took none to have any understanding" that was different from his own viewpoints, said one of his supporters, Roger North.[36] His favorite advisers were French Jesuit priests. James aroused considerable suspicion by having French advisers in the court, by having an alliance with Louis XIV, and by receiving gold from the French king.

Toward Catholicism and Absolutism

When the French ambassador to England pressured James to move faster to promote Catholicism, James complied. In August 1687 James issued his own Declaration of Indulgence, a paper that gave new rules concerning religious tolerance. James reversed the laws Parliament had passed during the reign of Charles II to prevent Catholics from holding office. The declaration went further to suspend all laws that affected religious practices. It did away with all religious tests. It allowed religious worship for all believers and forbade interference with any religious gathering. And it released all who had been imprisoned for religious nonconformity. To a twentieth-century ear, these rules sound like simple decency and common sense, but they defied laws passed by Parliament and were seen as a declaration of war against it. James went further. He gave permission to print Catholic writings and propaganda pamphlets. He simply dispensed with the Test Act, after which he gave offices and commissions to Catholics. Finally, he set up the Ecclesiastical Commission to punish Tories and Anglicans.

In a nation with deep prejudice against Catholics, these changes were shocking. Historian J. R. Jones describes prejudice against Catholics as the single most widespread and most powerful value. Every class of people in every section of the country feared Catholics and felt hostile toward them. The hostility had begun with Catholic persecutions in the 1550s. The relatively small population of Catholics in the seventeenth century could do little harm by themselves, but because they remained aloof from the Protestant population, they gave rise to great fear. Historian J. R. Jones says that "they occupied the same position as the Jews in twentieth-century eastern and central Europe; they were conveniently fitted into a conspiracy interpretation to explain current crises, and they were always available as scapegoats on whom attention could be directed and passions assuaged [relieved]."[37]

To succeed in his plan to bring England under Catholic control, James had to counter the strong anti-Catholic sentiment. He could only do that by controlling the courts and making Parliament submissive. James acted to control the courts first. He used his prerogative power to make Jeffreys the lord chancellor, the office in charge of appointing people to positions. James planned to have Jeffreys dismiss every judge who failed to act on James's behalf and install his own supporters instead. Then James took steps against local offices. He had a plan. He first appointed agents, called electoral intendants, who searched the local communities for elected officials who would support his Declaration of Indulgence and the repeal of the Test Act and religious laws. He planned to use loyal elected officials to help elect other like-minded candidates. The agents helped loyal officials by listing names, interests, and opinions of potential candidates. Because James had power over charters of local communities, he could force candidates to agree with his policies. Once he had his candidates elected to local offices, he planned to use the same political organization to elect favorable candidates to Parliament.

James's political strategy, though an effective plan, did not move forward according to schedule. Whig and Tory leaders saw that his campaign on the national level would produce a powerful Crown and a submissive Parliament. Aware of the king's intentions, Anglicans and Tories moved to enlist Puritan support by promising to pass acts of Toleration for Puritan worshipers later. By the summer of 1688 the Puritans had joined the Tories. Though Whigs and Tories foiled the plan James had devised for using agents to compile a bloc of sympathetic supporters, it was, nonetheless, a significant new technique in the development of politics.

As part of his plan to impose Catholicism on England, James appointed George Jeffreys (pictured) to unseat any judge who did not act on the king's behalf.

Intimidation of Protestants

To succeed at his plan to make England Catholic, James realized that he needed absolute power. He devised strategies to influence and intimidate Protestants. For example, he wanted to convert his Protestant daughters to assure a Catholic monarchy when he died. He wrote letters to Mary, wife of Prince William of Orange, asking her to turn Catholic. She refused. Converting his younger daughter, Anne, was even more important because she had children and could insure the Catholic line longer. Anne reportedly said that she would rather

James used intimidation to gain the absolute power he needed to be able to convert his nation to Catholicism.

Commission to "browbeat and bully bishops, clergymen and dons [teachers in the universities]," according to historian Trevelyan.[38] For example, in 1686 he suspended Anglican Henry Compton, the bishop of London, for refusing to suspend a clergyman. Then he used the court to attack universities, thinking he could control them. England's universities had a long tradition requiring students and teachers to abide by the rules of the Anglican Church. James offended tradition by installing a Catholic as president of Christ Church College at Oxford University. He tried to make Oxford's Magdalen College a seminary under the Catholic rule of an incompetent scholar named Bishop Parker. When Magdalen scholars refused to accept Bishop Parker as the leader of their college, James expelled those who objected and installed his candidate by force. Moreover, James sent an order to Cambridge University to accept a Benedictine monk as a student. The Cambridge vice chancellor refused, and Jeffreys bullied him for his refusal.

Further Intimidation

In another strategy of intimidation, James used Jeffreys and the Court of High Commission to punish political leaders and individuals who supported them. Those accused of participation in the plots against Charles II were hunted down and sent to the gallows, particularly Whigs. By law, two witnesses could condemn a man to death. Henry Cornish had been an alderman, or local official, and a sheriff and was a Whig and a Presbyterian. There was no evidence that he was involved in any

suffer death than to change her religion from Anglicanism to Catholicism. Other acts intimidated Protestants. James appointed a Catholic master of a school in the city of Bath. He used an Anglican college chapel in Oxford for Catholic vespers, or evening services. He gave annual salaries to Catholic bishops, making both Catholic and Anglican churches state supported. He turned Tories out of offices and replaced them with Catholics. He brought six Catholics to sit on the Privy Council and put Catholic officers in the army and the navy. Each act was one more irritation that frightened Protestants.

To intimidate Anglicans further, he used Jeffreys and the Court of High plot against Charles. When James hoped to find him guilty, only one witness could be found, but two years later, another witness, who was in need of James's approval, agreed to testify against Cornish. Macaulay explains the outcome:

> On the bench [sat] three judges who had been with Jeffreys in the West. . . . It is indeed but too true that the taste for blood is a taste which even men not naturally cruel may, by habit, speedily acquire. The bar and the bench united to browbeat the unfortunate Whig. The jury, named by a courtly Sheriff, readily found a verdict of Guilty; and, in spite of the indignant murmurs of the public, Cornish suffered death within ten days after he had been arrested.[39]

Another example of such punishing intimidation was the case made against Elizabeth Gaunt and John Fernley. James had decided to hunt down individuals who harbored rebels. Elizabeth Gaunt was a Baptist matron who used her wealth for acts of charity. She had helped James Burton, a man named in the fictitious Rye House plot, to board a boat for Amsterdam. After a time in exile, Burton returned and took refuge in the home of a poor barber, John Fernley. When one of James's officials offered a hundred-pound reward for the capture of James Burton, Fernley refused to betray him. But Burton gave himself up and testified against both Elizabeth Gaunt and John Fernley. They were convicted. Many people thought it impossible that the verdicts would be carried out, but James was without pity. Fernley was hanged, and Elizabeth Gaunt was burned alive at the stake.

The Revolt of Seven Bishops

James continued his strategies for absolute rule with little open resistance until the case of the seven bishops. The case began innocently enough. James had his 1687 Declaration of Indulgence reissued in the spring of 1688. He ordered the clergy to read the declaration in all churches in England—in London churches on May 20 or 27 and in churches outside London on June 3 or 10. Because the clergy knew that Parliament, not the king, was the source of law, they thought the declaration was illegal. They faced a dilemma: on one hand, they had long preached obedience to the king as a doctrine of the Anglican Church, but on the other hand, the king's declaration broke the law. Seven Anglican bishops solved the dilemma by taking a stand; they signed a petition on May 18 saying that they could not require the clergy to read the declaration. Archbishop of Canterbury William Sancroft asked James to reverse his decision. James was furious and accused the bishops of rebellion. On May 20 four London clergymen read the declaration; ninety-six did not. Two weeks later the clergy in the rest of the country refused to read it. When James ordered the seven bishops to trial, they refused to appear. James had them arrested and took them to the Tower of London while crowds, lined up on the streets, watched.

Before throngs of people at Westminster Hall on June 29, 1688, the seven bishops were publicly tried for seditious libel, or using false information to incite rebellion. When the jury returned a verdict of not guilty on June 30, the crowds in the streets broke into shouts. Wild mobs set

The Arrest and Trial of the Seven Bishops

In his book The English Revolution, *historian George Macaulay Trevelyan offers his thoughts on the scene as the bishops go to the Tower of London and the people react to their imprisonment and acquittal.*

"The Trial of the Seven Bishops, the greatest historical drama that ever took place before an authorized English law court, aroused popular feeling to its height. The sight of seven prelates [bishops] of blameless character and known loyalty to James . . . entering the Tower as prisoners and standing in the dock as culprits, showed as nothing else would have done that the most revered and the most loyal subjects in the land would be broken if they refused to become active parties to the King's illegal designs. If the Bishops suffered, who could hope to escape the royal vengeance? . . . The scene in Court after the acquittal, the day of furious joy in the streets of the capital, followed by a night of bonfires and of windows each illuminated with seven candles, the yet more ominous cheering of the King's own troops on Hounslow Heath, would have warned anyone but James that the ground was cracking under his feet."

fires in front of one of the king's palaces. Members of the nobility threw money to support a crowd burning an effigy of the pope. Bonfires burned all night around the city, and people displayed seven lighted candles in their windows. Even the king's military troops cheered and celebrated. The king's power had been called into question, and he was shattered by the news. He wanted to punish the bishops in spite of the verdict and to punish all the clergy who had refused to read the declaration, but such action would have declared war on the entire Church of England. The action was postponed.

Three weeks before the bishops' trial, James's second wife, Mary of Modena, had given birth to a son. Now the Catholic king had a Catholic heir to the throne, a son who would displace James's two adult, Protestant daughters, Mary and Anne. Since Mary, who had married James in 1672, had been childless for so long, Catholics thought the birth a miracle. But Protestants thought the Jesuit priests had sneaked in a baby as a plot to keep a Catholic on the throne. The birth heightened the political tension: a son gave the Whigs and the Tories a reason to plot a revolution, and a son gave James a new reason to be even more determined to have absolute power. Historian George Macaulay Trevelyan comments, "Thus, the Trial of the Seven Bishops and the birth of the Prince of Wales together ushered in the revolutionary period of James's reign."[40]

Plans for a Revolution

On June 30, after the bishops' trial, Protestant leaders decided to invite William of Orange, who was married to James's daughter Mary, to invade England. They felt that acting quickly was important because at the time feelings against James were strong and widespread. In addition, James was in the process of building his army with Irish Catholic soldiers, a change that frightened the English, who feared any army controlled by the king, especially one made up of Irish Catholics. Moreover, they could see no hope of relief since James was remodeling other branches of government to include more Catholics.

Seven Protestant leaders sent a letter inviting William to invade with a military force, and England would rally around him in rebellion against the government of James. The letter did not offer the

The trial of the seven bishops, shown walking to their trial, incited widespread feelings of rebellion against James.

Crown to William, nor did it say what the settlement might be. The letter was signed by representatives of different parties: by the duke of Devonshire, Admiral Edward Russell, and Henry Sidney for the Whigs; by the earl of Danby, and Bishop Henry Compton of London for the Anglican Church and the Tory Party; and by the earl of Shrewsbury and Lord Lumley as Protestants who were recently converted. Signing the letter was an act of treason against their own government; it meant that these men took their lives and their fortunes into their hands for the sake of

---

English Reaction to Irish Troops

James's decision to supply his army with Irish troops aroused the passions of English people. At the time, hatred of the Irish ran high. In volume two of The History of England, *Thomas Babington Macaulay describes the feelings of the people.*

"He brought over Irishmen, not indeed enough to hold down the single city of London, or the single county of York, but more than enough to excite the alarm and rage of the whole kingdom. . . .

Of the many errors which James committed, none was more fatal than this. . . . Not even the arrival of a brigade of Lewis's [Louis XIV's] musketeers would have excited such resentment and shame as our ancestors felt when they saw armed columns of Papists [Catholics], just arrived from Dublin, moving in military pomp along the high roads. No man of English blood then regarded the aboriginal [native] Irish as his countrymen. They did not belong to our branch of the great human family. They were distinguished from us by more than one moral and intellectual peculiarity. . . . They had an aspect of their own, a mother tongue of their own. . . . They were therefore foreigners; and of all foreigners they were the most hated and despised; the most hated, for they had, during five centuries, always been our enemies; the most despised, for they were our vanquished, enslaved, and most despoiled [ravaged] enemies. . . . Yet it is certain that, in the seventeenth century, they were generally despised in our island as both a stupid and a cowardly people. And these were the men who were to hold England down by main force while her civil and ecclesiastical [church-related] constitution was destroyed. The blood of the whole nation boiled at the thought."

their nation. The invitation was carried to Holland by Admiral Arthur Herbert, disguised as a common sailor.

William agreed to the invasion. Ever since the bishops' trial and the birth of James's son, William had been thinking about a possible invasion. William made his reply in a declaration. In it he said that he had three goals, which were to rid the nation of arbitrary and lawless power supported by a military force, to restore laws dating back to the Magna Carta, and to restore the authority of a freely elected Parliament. He made no mention of whether to keep or dethrone James because that issue would arouse debate and divide the nation. All that was necessary was to say that a free Parliament should decide all matters in dispute. In previous letters to English political leaders, William had already made it known that he favored freedom of religious worship for all, but he did not favor repeal of the Test Act or the admission of Catholics to office. The first of these opinions appealed to the Whigs, and the second to the Tories and Anglicans; therefore, his declaration offered maximum opportunity for strong, unified support.

Fearing that a Catholic England was inevitable under King James, Protestant leaders asked William of Orange (pictured) to invade England.

Preparations Move Forward

William had several difficulties to overcome before he could invade. First, he had to obtain the unanimous consent of the Dutch state. Unanimous consent was difficult because any one of the seven Dutch provinces or any city within any province had the right to veto the use of the army and navy. By chance, William got unexpected help from Louis XIV of France, who made two moves that solidified support for William. First, Louis had insulted and bullied the Dutch so much that even William's opposition rallied to his side. Second, Louis withdrew forces that had been threatening Holland because he wanted to use them against the Germans. With the French forces gone, Holland would be safer while the Dutch troops were invading England. The Dutch states unanimously agreed to send William to win an alliance with England. William needed four million Dutch gulden from the state for military needs. He had to recruit nine thousand sailors for the Dutch navy and man two armies—one to invade and one to guard his home state in the event of French aggression. William worried about fighting a war on two fronts; he hoped from the start "for a bloodless success in England," according

Communication Across the Channel

During the reign of James II, information passed between Prince William of Orange and English government leaders. In The Revolution of 1688 in England, *J. R. Jones describes how the secret correspondence traveled.*

"At the Dutch end it was managed by Bentinck, helped by Dijkvelt and Zuylestein. In England the leading part was played by Henry Sidney, 'the great wheel on which the Revolution rolled'. . . .

It is no exaggeration to say that the whole success of William's English policies, and the Revolution itself, depended entirely on these four men. . . . Certainly they had no difficulty in deceiving James and his ministers and in preserving almost total secrecy in their work in 1687–8. . . .

In the earlier stages most letters were sent by the ordinary post, to genuine addresses in England and Holland, from which they were then to be forwarded. . . . Ciphers [codes] were never used in open letters. Instead key words, or devices such as ending a postscript with an 'etc.', indicated that the blank portions of letters contained passages written in white, or invisible ink. . . .

As tension increased in 1688 . . . letters were sent by ordinary merchant ships sailing between London and Amsterdam and Rotterdam. . . .

In the final stages before the invasion, when speed was essential and secrecy of paramount importance, fast yachts and small vessels operated special courier services."

to historian Ashley.[41] Before working out his strategy, he sent Dutch fishing boats to the English coast to collect intelligence. He sent his adviser, E. van Weede Dijkvelt, to spy out the land and get topographical information.

By September 1688 everyone, including James, knew the Dutch preparations in the ports would be directed against the English government. James was alarmed enough now to make concessions. He promised to uphold laws and call Parliament. He promised to reverse all his acts against Anglicans, university dons, and Protestants. He assured the Dutch that he had no secret treaty with France. But he did not promise to remove Catholics from the army or to stop removing Protestants and installing Catholics in other offices. By now the nation's anger and distrust were at their height and not to be dispelled by the king's concessions. Too much had been done in three years to be forgotten on James's word now.

Rebellion Spreads

As the days wore on, rebellion spread. The earl of Feversham, commander in chief of James's army, ordered soldiers to stop performing their work. The lieutenant general headed a secret conspiracy to turn troops to William's side. Anne publicly joined with the church and the nation against her father. Bishops refused to support the king and speak against the rebellion. In early November William's declaration was printed and distributed on the streets. A ballad about "an Orange," Prince William, became popular. Throughout the country people waited in a mood of skepticism, caution, and anger to see what was forthcoming.

While William made preparations and gathered forces, it was necessary to watch closely for political changes in England and to keep James deceived as much as possible about the meaning of William's actions. James was told that the Dutch readied their troops because they feared an alliance between James and Louis XIV and would invade if James made one. When James asked what Anglican men would do, the earl of Clarendon told him that they would behave themselves like honest men, a true but deceptive answer. To the Spanish ambassador James reportedly said that he would either win everything or lose it all. It appeared that James would remain determined not to compromise. James had only a few ministers left by his side—only Jeffreys and his adviser, Jesuit priest Sir Edward Petre, "the two most unpopular men in the island," according to Trevelyan; he had driven the others away.[42] By his unyielding determination to reinstate Catholicism and his stubborn determination to rule absolutely, James had, in essence, contributed to the rebellion against him.

Chapter

5 From Invasion to Rights, 1688–1689

Prince William invaded England in the last months of 1688. Several conditions came together to give the invasion the good fortune of success. Even unexpected chance events and accidents were overcome or turned to advantage. By fall all classes of English society anticipated William's arrival. Parliamentary leaders attended to details in London and on the coast. William managed problems and concerns both at home and in England. Even James, with his rigid beliefs and collapse of will, unintentionally helped to make the operation go smoothly.

After the bishops' trial and the birth of James's son, all classes in English society united against James and in favor of William. Commoners had already opposed James by joining Monmouth in 1685 and later by opposing the king's election strategy of using local officials, many of whom were common people, to help him pack Parliament. The gentry and rising merchant class approved of the invasion because they thought it respectable, since William, married to a Stuart princess, was in charge. The Tories and the army officers, who could have sabotaged the plan, approved because James had lost their loyalty. Royalist Sir John Reresby wrote in his memoirs: "It is very strange . . . that neither the gentry nor the common people

seemed much afeared or concerned at [the invasion], saying, the Prince comes only to maintain the Protestant religion; he will do England no harm."[43]

Preparation and Waiting

In the days leading up to the invasion, parliamentary leaders managed events in the capital and made preparations on the coast. They continued to monitor the actions of the king and to use every opportunity to deceive him about William's obvious preparations. James Johnstone and Henry Sidney, two of the invasion organizers, used their connections with Whigs to keep Whigs and Tories united. They used their connections with Anglican clergy, army officers, and members of court to keep all parties informed and calm while William prepared. Uncertain where William would land or what James's forces would do, leaders had to be ready in more than one place. A fleet of forty-eight English ships docked at Dartmouth in the southwest. Conspirators, who thought William would most likely land on the east coast, gathered at York to await his arrival. Every day the English put up a finger to test for a favorable east wind to blow William across the Channel. The waiting dragged on through September and the first weeks of October.

William, for whom the risks were very great, analyzed conditions and made careful preparations for an invasion that historian J. R. Jones calls "preposterously rash."[44] By taking an army and a fleet to invade England, he left his own country less protected, even though he thought Louis XIV, his greatest worry, was safely occupied in battles in Germany. The possibility existed, however, that the French might interpret the invasion as an English-Dutch alliance threatening to the French, who would, in turn, then act aggressively toward the Dutch and France's other neighbors. William could not afford such dangers just to save English freedoms; his letters explaining his plans assured Dutch deputies that the risk was worth helping the English convene a free Parliament to secure the Protestant religion from a Catholic takeover.

Further Risks

Besides attending to the risks at home, William also attended to risks in England. William depended on his political connections in England and his own tiny group of advisers to gather, evaluate, and communicate information. He had to trust their accuracy and integrity; because a mistaken report or a leaked secret could be costly, William was very careful with messages that crossed the Channel. Another risk involved James's large, strong army, which was much larger than the forces William could take. Though he thought that James's army would desert the king and come over to his side, he would be certain only after he landed. As a precaution, he sent English army officers a letter. In it he argued that a victory for James would enslave the nation and ruin Protestantism. Under those conditions, James could make army officers disposable, and they could lose their positions or even their lives; therefore, they should remember to place their allegiance to James beneath their obligation "to God and Religion, Country, Selves, Posterity."[45] Finally, because the English Channel is particularly stormy late in the year, William risked the danger of losing ships in bad weather. Consequently, he tried to make plans for alternate landings on the English shores in case a storm arose.

As William (pictured) made preparations and gathered forces to invade England, all classes of English society anticipated his arrival.

Historians seem uncertain what motivated William to take these risks. William did believe in predestination, the belief that God had events already planned. Thinking the invasion to be God's will, William felt confident he would succeed in saving the English and Scottish nations. Some thought luck was on his side. J. R. Jones disagrees. He says, "William's decisions developed out of a shrewd analysis of a constantly changing situation, and his success was based on a masterly exploitation of every favorable circumstance."[46]

As others prepared and waited, James panicked. His belief in God's intervention and in his own rightness had blinded him to reality until it was too late. Believing that God was on his side, he still could not believe that his son-in-law would lead an invasion against him, and he refused to declare war on the Dutch or demand French help. His inability or refusal to see reality had already lost him many opportunities to win support, opportunities that could not be reversed at such a late date. He had neglected English army officers and brought in Irish soldiers. He had delayed a strategy for dividing Whigs and Tories until it was too late. He had favored his French ministers until the country believed all ministers were mere French puppets. He could change none of these conditions when he finally realized that the north was rising against him and his army officers were in secret league with William. In his panic James offered to make the same concessions that had been refused before—to cancel arrests, to extend pardons, to restore fellows at Magdalen College, to restore justices. The doubting English thought his concessions were insincere and that James would reverse them should William fail to invade. In his *Maxims of State*, the marquis of Halifax said: "A people may let a King fall, yet still remain a people: but if a King let his people slip from him, he is no longer King."[47]

William Sets Sail

Finally, on October 19 William and his armada set sail. He set out with fifty warships, five hundred transport ships, five hundred cavalry soldiers, and eleven thousand infantry soldiers. He had given orders that his warships were to protect the transport ships from any interference from the English fleet, but they were to avoid battle if at all possible. Soon after his fleet got into the Channel, an unexpected storm came up. The whole invasion force had to turn back. The storm caused the loss of some of his horses, but no men were lost. Determined to go through with the invasion, William collected more horses and prepared to leave again as soon as the weather permitted.

The fleet was ready by October 28, and the Channel had calmed. On Thursday, November 1, William signaled to Admiral Arthur Herbert, the leader of the fleet, to put out to sea as soon as wind permitted and to sail toward a landing on the northeastern coast. By the afternoon of November 2, the wind blew with such ferocity from the east that the fleet was unable to turn north to land at York. In fog that protected the fleet from being seen, William gave orders to change direction and sail for a port in the southwest. By the time the fleet reached the Strait of Dover, the sky was sunny. Crowds, having sighted the ships, gathered on the white cliffs to watch the procession. According to histo-

William's fleet braves fierce winds and dense fog on its journey to the shores of England.

rian Maurice Ashley, a London newspaper reported that the fleet looked "like a thick forest." Prince William hoisted a banner that read "For the Protestant Religion and Liberty," and the navy fired cannons in salute as the ships passed Dover.[48]

The Bloodless Revolution Happens

William and his armada landed at the port of Torbay in Cornwall on November 5; William stepped ashore, and his soldiers disembarked. They met no resistance, but neither did they have a reception to welcome them. The seven men who had invited William and signed the letter waited in other places: three in the north at York, the bishop in London, and the remaining three on their way to Torbay to meet William. By the evening of November 9, William had unloaded his ships and had set up headquarters in Exeter, just north of Torbay. The Exeter city magistrates, who feared losing their jobs, were hostile, but the citizens of the town gave William a thunderous welcome. William, whose success depended entirely on his ability to exploit the defections from James's army, found that soldiers and officers defected just as had been anticipated. On November 16 a deluge of soldiers began to appear, the first group of officers arriving from Salisbury. Then regiments of officers came from Oxford. At the same time, most of the gentry from the western part of the country rallied to William's side.

James assembled his army at Salisbury, a city to the northeast of Exeter. On November 19 James personally joined his troops for seven days, thinking most of them might remain loyal if he led them himself. But he found the army camp disorganized and the soldiers demoralized. During his first night there, two officers and four hundred soldiers deserted to William. James could still have launched an attack on William with the remaining forces, but he hesitated. After reviewing his troops, James broke down physically and psychologically and had to remain secluded. Repeated nosebleeds disabled him, and he was unable to sleep. Then he ordered a retreat. Soldiers continued to defect, and James had no way to stop them. The order for a retreat marked the beginning of the end.

When William did not land in York, the three waiting conspirators revised their plans and decided to take the county of Yorkshire. In a bloodless coup the earl of Danby, one of the conspirators, and his associates took control of the city of York first. Historian Trevelyan explains: "The militia, gentry and populace . . . were unanimous, and Danby led them with such ability and cunning that no resistance was put up by the King's servants and soldiers in the garrison towns."[49] Within ten days the men had taken the cities of Nottingham, Leicester, Carlisle, Newcastle, Gloucester, Norwich, King's Lynn, and Derby. This takeover in the northeast meant that James had no place left to go, a development that further demoralized him.

Tories and Whigs gradually gathered at Exeter, where the two parties joined together into one party. Sir Edward Seymour, a Tory leader in the west country,

James reacts as though his defeat is a foregone conclusion when he receives the news that William's fleet has landed.

The Prince Enters Exeter

In The History of England, *volume two, Thomas Babington Macaulay describes the response of the local people as Prince William approached Exeter.*

"The houses were gaily decorated. Doors, windows, balconies, and roofs were thronged with gazers. An eye accustomed to the pomp of war would have found much to criticize in the spectacle. For several toilsome marches in the rain, through roads where one who travelled on foot sank at every step up to the ankles in clay [mud], had not improved the appearance either of the men or of their accoutrements [equipment]. But the people of Devonshire, altogether unused to the splendour of well ordered camps, were overwhelmed with delight and awe. Descriptions of the martial pageant were circulated all over the kingdom. . . . Surrounded by a goodly company of gentlemen and pages, was borne aloft the Prince's banner. On its broad folds the crowd which covered the roofs and filled the windows read with delight that memorable inscription, 'The Protestant religion and the liberties of England.' But the acclamations redoubled when, attended by forty running footmen, the Prince himself appeared, armed on back and breast, wearing a white plume and mounted on a white charger. . . . Once those grave features relaxed into a smile. It was when an ancient woman, perhaps one of the zealous Puritans, . . . broke from the crowd, rushed through the drawn swords and curvetting [prancing] horses, touched the hand of the deliverer, and cried out that now she was happy."

proposed that they sign an association, an informal agreement. Its purpose was to bind their unity in order to pursue the points of William's declaration and to stand by William and by each other against loss of their religious liberties. Begun as an informal agreement between Whigs and Tories in Exeter, the association grew to include the signatures of a great majority of Englishmen. It remained in effect until William had successfully achieved his goals.

William's invasion had had a successful beginning. His armada had landed safely, the army had come to his side, and Whigs, Tories, and local residents had gathered to support him. His next plan was to go to London. Since he had too few horses and the roads were muddy, he planned to leave heavy equipment and

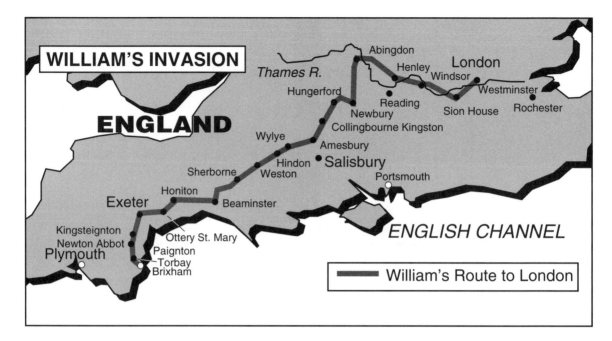

WILLIAM'S INVASION

ENGLAND

Thames R.

Abingdon
Henley
London
Windsor
Hungerford
Reading
Westminster
Newbury
Sion House
Rochester
Collingbourne Kingston
Wylye
Amesbury
Hindon
Salisbury
Sherborne
Weston
Portsmouth
Honiton
Exeter
Beaminster
Kingsteignton
Newton Abbot
Ottery St. Mary
Plymouth
Paignton
Torbay
Brixham

ENGLISH CHANNEL

William's Route to London

much of his baggage at Exeter. William planned to make a slow, deliberate trip to London. In the event that small groups of rebels might oppose him, he wanted to allow enough time for any such opposition to crumble.

England Without a Government

After failing to lead his own army, James returned to London on November 26 to bad news. His daughter Anne had deserted him. Even more demoralizing than being forsaken by his own children, James finally realized that all he had left was time and a chance to save himself and his family. In an attempt to gain time, James sent the earl of Halifax, the earl of Nottingham, and the earl of Godolphin, three moderates, to negotiate with William to

plan elections and summon a free Parliament. William quickly identified the plan as nothing but a smoke screen and rejected the negotiations. James then sent his wife and his infant son to France. Alone on December 11, James decided to leave in the early hours of December 12. He left Whitehall Palace by a secret door to go to Kent to get on a yacht and sail to France. Before leaving, he destroyed his September call for a new Parliament and left orders for the army to be disbanded. He was hoping to leave England in a state of anarchy, fantasizing that a repentant English people would summon him and he would return victorious, leading a French army. As soon as the earl of Dartmouth, commander of the navy, heard that James had left, he turned the navy over to William. "Thus five weeks after the Dutch fleet had anchored in Torbay the bloodless—and therefore glorious—Revolution appeared to have been completed," comments historian Maurice Ashley.[50]

When England awakened on December 12, the country had no government and again faced the danger of anarchy, as it had twenty years earlier, when the army ousted Richard Cromwell. The greatest danger was the possibility that mobs would attack Catholics and that small disorders would escalate into a general attack on all wealthy families. That night mobs did burn a few Catholic homes and chapels, but no lives were lost. In quick response, the aristocrat and gentry classes united and temporarily reestablished order.

The successful accomplishment of William's invasion, however, had a minor misfortune. By chance a party of armed sailors and fishermen captured James near Kent on his way to France. James was allowed to go back to Whitehall, where a few people cheered his return. During the night of December 18, a delegation of Tories woke James to help him make a second departure. This time they took him to Rochester, a town on the southeast coast. On December 21 James vanished during the night. He began his journey by yacht and ended it on one of Louis XIV's frigates, which took him safely to France.

William Takes Over

On December 18 William arrived in London, and events moved quickly. Before Christmas, a representative gathering of Whigs and Tories met and asked William to take over administration. Since by law only a king can call a regular Parliament, they asked William to summon a Convention Parliament, a temporary legislative body, to serve until a regular Parliament could be called. William sent letters for its meeting on January 22, 1689. Then he turned to administrative tasks, careful to combine firmness with moderation. Since anti-Catholic riots had not entirely ceased, he immediately quelled the anarchy and protected Catholics from violence. Then, turning to the needs of state, he borrowed money from banks in London to pay for expenses. He confirmed the authority of magistrates and law courts, which had lapsed when James departed. He dismissed Catholic officers from the army, rallied the rest, and sent Irish troops home. And he took precautions to prevent the French from helping James return. Legally, he had no authority to take these measures, but there was no other government, and people obeyed him.

Even though William's letters calling for election of members to the Convention Parliament were technically improper, the people accepted them as valid. Citizens rose to the occasion and conducted elections with "sober patriotism," says historian Trevelyan. Neither party attempted to influence voters, and neither party engaged in bitter conflict or rancor. Historian Trevelyan observes, "Never was a general election so free of government influence as that which returned the House of Commons of 1689."[51] Most areas of the country voted for candidates who were pro-William. Overwhelmingly, the people voted for Protestants.

The Convention, which met in January, had serious issues on its agenda. Members essentially started with nothing—no monarch, no official Parliament, and a destroyed constitution—but Whigs and Tories, guided more by common sense now than by party prejudice, had past experience to instruct them. The problem of a successor to the throne was the most obvious item to address, but they put that issue aside. Before they could decide who the next monarch would be and offer the Crown, they needed to decide on the distribution of power between the monarch and Parliament and the constitutional place of the Church of England. Members began their work by listing grievances against James II, a task that fostered debate and clarified opinions. In the process the Convention Parliament identified many issues that would eventually have to be addressed by a regular Parliament. Within a month the Convention Parliament had accomplished what this temporary body could do—name a successor.

Considerable debate surrounded the issue of a successor to the throne. Both Whigs and Tories wanted William to be the king; the differences occurred over the basis for making him king. On one side of the argument was the consideration of divine right, long an important point for Tories and the Anglican clergy, but by leaving the throne and going to France, James had made hereditary solutions unworkable. One possibility was to recall James with conditions, but he would accept none. Another was to make William a regent in James's name, but that plan would make England a republic of France since James now lived there. Another was to declare

The Emotions of the Revolution

In The Glorious Revolution of 1688, *Maurice Ashley offers insight into the strong emotions that surrounded the Revolution.*

"'The people,' observed the Marquis of Halifax sagely, 'can seldom agree to move together against a government, but they can sit still and see it undone.' That is what many Englishmen, though not all, did in the crucial months of November and December 1688. Respect was still felt for the person of the King but long pent-up emotions were released and anti-papist rioting took place not merely in London but in many other parts of England. A story survives that before James finally left Whitehall 'he looked out of the window and saw the violence and fierceness of the rabble,' and said, 'I cannot help or hinder it, God alone can do it.' While awaiting the arrival of William of Orange at St. James's Palace, a Londoner was writing, 'we all pray [he] may come quickly that a stop may be put to the fury of the rabble who have done great mischief.' Lack of an adequate police force and the rapid dispersal of the royal army were enough to make respectable people tremble for their goods and their lives."

Mary the queen and William the prince consort, or spouse and partner of a monarch, but Mary refused to be queen unless William could be king, and William refused to be prince or king consort.

On the other side of the argument, the Whigs wanted to change the order of succession even though a change killed the idea of divine hereditary right. Whigs suggested making the title to the Crown a parliamentary title, not a divine title. This way the monarchy would never get out of hand as it had with James; with a divine title, a monarch could always override a human Parliament. The Whigs argued that both monarch and Parliament should have human authority. With this plan Parliament could declare the throne vacant and fill it by an act to be voted on. The Tories finally adopted the Whig plan. The convention drafted the following formula, quoted by historian Trevelyan:

That King James the Second, having endeavored to subvert the Constitution of the Kingdom, by breaking the *Original Contract* between King and people (a Whig remark), and by the advice of Jesuits and other wicked persons [Catholics] having violated the fundamental laws and withdrawn himself out of the Kingdom, hath *abdicated* the government (a concession to the Tories) and that *the throne is thereby vacant* (a Whig conclusion).[52]

The Crown and Power Passed to a New Reign

Before offering the joint Crown to William and Mary, Parliament set down the conditions for their rule. Completed in three weeks, the Declaration of Right, as the conditions were called, listed thirteen points that restored, renewed, and protected existing rights. The earl of Halifax, as spokesman for Parliament, interviewed William and Mary in Whitehall on February 13, 1689. He offered them the Crown and the Declaration of Right at the same time, and they accepted both. This Parliament also set up rules for future succession to the throne. The last business having to do with succession established the oath that members of new Parliament would swear to the Crown. It read simply: "I A. B. [any member of Parliament] do sincerely promise and swear, That I will be faithful, and bear true allegiance, to their Majesties, King William and Queen Mary."[53] Three months later Scotland also offered the Crown to William and Mary on May 11, 1689. The short-term Revolution was complete.

The events of the Glorious Revolution had taken place within three months, from the landing of William in early November to his acceptance of the Crown with his wife Mary in mid-February. By rejecting James II, the English had reasserted that no power could limit the people's constitutional rights and liberties, as James had done. By accepting King William III and Queen Mary II, the English had reasserted their desire for a monarch, but only one that honored their rights. The long-term glory of the Revolution, however, still lay ahead in the Revolution Settlement and the peace that followed. Historian J. R. Jones tells why he believes this bloodless revolution was remarkable:

The speed and bloodlessness of the Revolution in England, the near unanimity

The Crown Offered to William and Mary

In The History of England, *volume two, Thomas Babington Macaulay describes the scene in Whitehall Palace when the marquis of Halifax offered the crown to William and Mary.*

"On the morning of Wednesday, the thirteenth of February, the court of Whitehall and all the neighbouring streets were filled with gazers. The magnificent Banqueting House, the masterpiece of [architect] Inigo [Jones], embellished by masterpieces of Rubens, had been prepared for a great ceremony. The walls were lined by the yeomen of the guard. Near the northern door, on the right hand, a large number of Peers had assembled. On the left were the Commons with their Speaker, attended by the mace [the symbol of authority of a legislative body]. The southern door opened: and the Prince and Princess of Orange, side by side, entered, and took their place under the canopy of state.

Both Houses approached bowing low. William and Mary advanced a few steps. Halifax on the right, and Powle on the left, stood forth; and Halifax spoke. The Convention, he said, had agreed to a resolution which he prayed Their Highnesses to hear. They signified their assent: and the clerk of the House of Lords read, in a loud voice, the Declaration of Right. When he had concluded, Halifax, in the name of all the Estates of the Realm, requested the Prince and Princess to accept the crown.

William, in his own name and in that of his wife, answered that the crown was, in their estimation, the more valuable because it was presented to them as a token of the confidence of the nation. 'We thankfully accept,' he said, 'what you have offered us.'"

of the formerly hostile Whig and Tory parties in support of the main parts of the Settlement, are all the more remarkable when set (as they must be) against the background of chronic political crisis, instability and lack of mutual trust which characterized the period after the Restoration [period following 1660 when Charles was restored as king].[54]

6 From Rights to Settlement, 1689–1702

After crowning William and Mary, Parliament and the English upper classes enacted the Revolution Settlement. The violence and abuses of the past led them toward a more democratic government, a system that marks a point between a constitutional monarchy and a constitutional democracy. The Revolution Settlement, the collection of changes in the structure of English government, took place throughout the reign of William and Mary. It set forth procedures that secured the principles of the Magna Carta and extended the people's rights even further.

The Bill of Rights

The first act of the new king and queen was to convert the temporary Convention into an official Parliament. Though composed of the same members, Parliament made official the Declaration of Right, signed by William and Mary before they were crowned, and changed its name to the Bill of Rights. This act clarified the powers of the monarch and Parliament. The whole process, which clarified other functions of government, became the Revolution Settlement.

Newly defined, the monarch had stated limitations. All future monarchs were to be members of the Church of England. The Bill of Rights prohibited the monarch from unilaterally—or acting alone—suspending the laws of the land and levying money—collecting taxes—without the consent of Parliament. Moreover, the Bill of Rights stated that the monarch must convene Parliament frequently and allow its members the right of free speech. The monarch was responsible for foreign and domestic policy and had the right to act along with the House of Commons and the House of Lords in making and changing laws. On the other hand, Parliament, which now had a stronger role than in the past, was chiefly responsible for making and passing laws and managing the nation's money. Though these rules had appeared in earlier reigns, none of the Stuart kings had signed a document agreeing to them, as William and Mary had.

Once the Settlement made clear that the law was above the king, it became important to have an independent judicial system, independent of both the monarch and Parliament. James II had been able to break laws because he had the power to appoint Jeffreys and to pack the courts with his favored appointees, thus avoiding punishment. In one of his first freely taken executive actions, William stated that judges could not be removed from their positions as long as they behaved properly. The Settlement finally decided on the rule that the Crown could not remove a judge from office unless both houses of Parliament made a request for removal. Moreover, William took a more humane and fair attitude toward the accused, an attitude supported by Whigs and Tories. The Bill of Rights stated, for example, that the courts could not set excessive bail, the amount of money an accused person puts up to assure that he or she will appear in court and not escape. In the reorganized system the judges, independent of the lawmakers, could interpret cases according to legal standards set by the laws. Historian George Macaulay Trevelyan comments: "The law was made arbiter of all issues by its own legal standards, without fear of what Government could do either to Judge or to Juries. It is difficult to exaggerate the importance of this as a step towards real justice and civilization."[55]

Settling Religious Conflicts

After a century of vicious fighting among religions, Parliament revised religious laws. Many statesmen who criticized the practice of religious persecution spoke of the damage it had caused. Trade had suffered because Puritan manufacturers and merchants were persecuted. Besides, the public found persecuting Protestants embarrassing. The earl of Nottingham, an Anglican member of the monarch's advisory council, introduced the Toleration Act in Parliament in May 1689. This act made several changes. It allowed freedom of public worship to all groups that accepted the doctrine, or belief in principles, of Trinity—belief in God as Father, Son, and Holy Spirit—and agreed that the Bible was divinely inspired. In addition, it allowed freedom of worship to all who rejected both the idea of the pope's su-

As their first act as king and queen, William and Mary established the Bill of Rights, which limited the power of monarchs.

premacy and transubstantiation, the doctrine that the bread and wine of the Eucharist are transformed into the body and blood of Jesus, although their appearances remain the same. There was a special act for Baptists, who were permitted to delay baptism of their members until they reached maturity. In practice this act excluded Catholics and Unitarians, but it gave freedom of worship to non-Anglican Protestants.

Some of the old laws concerning religion remained the same. All Dissenters, or non-Anglicans, were still banned from universities. Catholics were excluded from holding office in all parts of government, national and local. Protestant Dissenters were eligible to hold a seat in Parliament or public office if they received the sacrament according to Anglican rule as set down in the *Book of Common Prayer*, and Puritans could still vote. When Parliament dropped the punishments of the Clarendon Code, all Dissenters benefited; ministers like John Bunyan were no longer jailed, and fines were lifted for those who did not attend church. Catholics benefited too. For a decade priests were allowed to say mass in homes without punishment so long as they disguised their role while in public; in 1699, however, Tories tightened the laws again and forbade Catholic mass in homes and Catholic education for children.

William, who was brought up as a Dissenter, was more tolerant than English Anglicans and disliked all the bigotry and prejudice. He wanted to treat all Protestants equally and abolish rules barring them from public office. He also wanted better treatment for Catholics because he found it difficult to make alliances with Catholic countries when his own country oppressed Catholics. Parliament, however, prevailed. The religious settlement of 1689 was a compromise between Tories and Whigs, somewhat favorable to the Tories and Anglicans. Historian Trevelyan says, "The Toleration Act has proved one of the most lastingly successful measures ever passed by Parliament" because it ended religious wars in England, perhaps having saved the nation from another civil war.[56] At the end of the seventeenth century, England had more tolerant religious laws than any European country except Holland, and these laws prevailed in England for more than a century.

The Machinery of Representative Government

Parliament's first work after the Revolution had been to define the roles of the three branches of representative government—the executive, legislative, and judicial branches—and to settle the religious wars. As the reign of William and Mary continued, English leaders developed several institutions necessary to make representative government function.

One institution was the council of ministers, the Privy Council, a number of men who advised the king and queen and carried out administrative tasks. All kings had advisers. Because William was more interested in foreign affairs than domestic affairs, his appointed ministers ran affairs at home. Consequently, the ministers, the Privy Council, became an important part of the government. Unlike the previous days, when a king's advisers were personal favorites or flatterers looking for favors from a generous king, William appointed conscientious men to manage domestic policy. William appointed the earl of Danby as lord president, two secretaries of state, a lord of the purse, or treasury, and others. The Privy Council was the beginning of the institution that developed into the ministries in England and functions somewhat like the president's cabinet in American government. To be fair, William at first tried to appoint both Whig and Tory ministers, but he found that too many arguments arose. He discovered that Parliament and the administration worked best when the ministers on the Privy Council came from the party that had a majority in the House of Commons. The Revolution Settlement stated that no foreigners could sit either in Parliament or on the Privy Council.

During William and Mary's reign the political-party system became more important. When William decided that the Privy Council should be of the same party as the majority party in Parliament, both parties saw that electing a majority of representatives to the House of Commons gave them power to affect economic policy. Thus, the middle class and gentry learned to participate and be active in elections. The parties learned how to campaign by using James II's strategy of identifying lists of supporters and potential candidates and by using newspapers and pamphlets to inform and persuade the voters.

A Balance of Powers

Political parties had developed gradually in England. During William and Mary's reign with a more powerful Parliament, the two parties, the Whigs and the Tories,

competed for control and kept Parliament from becoming as powerful as the former king had been. Historian George Macaulay Trevelyan explains:

> For the Revolution Settlement of 1689 was not the triumph of a party, but an agreement of the two chief parties to live and let live. The balance of Whig and Tory, each jealous of the other and both jealous of the Crown, serve to protect the liberties of the individual Englishmen from the onslaughts of power.[57]

With the memory of two periods of anarchy during which it appeared that England might come under military control, the Settlement Parliament took measures to prevent the nation from ever becoming a military dictatorship. Both Whigs and Tories remembered the days when the army overthrew Richard Cromwell and no government existed and the days when James II increased his army with Irish soldiers in his march toward absolute power. In 1689 Parliament passed the Mutiny Act. It stated that Parliament controlled the army during wartime and that no standing army could exist during peacetime without the consent of Parliament; that is, the military would be under civil control. To maintain control, Parliament took charge of allocating military funds.

During the Revolution Settlement the House of Commons took over all government finances. During the Tudor and Stuart reigns, Parliament usually granted the monarchs funds for life. After the Revolution, William and the Privy Council ministers had to ask Commons for money each year for the king's personal use and for specified purposes. Commons set up committees to review the requests and oversee

The London Stock Exchange, opened during the reign of William and Mary, helped strengthen English economy and government.

the accounts. On the committees' recommendations, Parliament either did or did not grant funds. Thus, ministers, treasury officials, and members of Parliament worked together on monetary policy.

A New Monetary System

Under the reorganized system Parliament borrowed, not the king. As the new monetary policy went into effect, a more elaborate banking system developed. Individual bankers, who now lent to the government at 8 percent, organized themselves into a group that become the Bank of England after it was granted a charter in 1694. In that year the bank's notes, which were backed by savings deposits and could be paid in gold, became legal tender; that is, the notes were the first genuine paper money in England. Then the government redesigned coins to make them more durable. Using both paper money and coins, England had a sound currency system. Two other developments contributed to the complex monetary system. In 1688 Edward Lloyd originated an insurance company; today the company is known simply as Lloyd's. And in 1698 the London Stock Exchange opened, a system for organizing the supply of money so that companies and businesses could borrow and grow. A representative government needs a steady and secure supply of money; it depends on money from capitalists, the providers and managers of money. Together the House of Commons and the financial institutions have kept English

The National Debt

In The English Revolution 1688–1689, *historian George Macaulay Trevelyan explains the importance of the financial institutions that supported the English government after the Revolution. The system made English kings richer than all their rivals.*

"Government borrowing on Parliament security, the National Debt, and the Bank of England founded in 1694, these were the methods and institutions that enabled England to defeat France and enlarge her Empire as much by the purse as by the sword; without Lord Treasurer Godolphin, Marlborough could not have won his wars [a series of bloody European battles that defeated French troops]; and without the financial support of the City and the House of Commons all Pitt's genius would not have won Canada and India. . . . Generation after generation we find City magnates, many of whom were Dissenters, opening their purses to the secure investment of the National Debt guaranteed by Parliament, to support Governments they trusted."

government strong and stable from the reign of William and Mary to the present.

The Revolution Settlement secured another very important institution in a representative government—freedom of the press. Freedom of the press means the right to print and publish "matter obnoxious to the Government of the day," reports historian Trevelyan.[58] In order to guard against an undisciplined press that could otherwise become a nuisance or cause harm, sedition and libel were made crimes. Sedition is the publication of language that ignites a rebellion. Libel is the publication of false information that damages a person's reputation. Although those are the only two legal restrictions, social custom and public opinion ordinarily place pressure on authors and publishers to uphold standards of decency as the current society defines them. The parliamentary debates over freedom of the press in 1695 led to the common law of England regarding freedom of speech. This law allowed the executive branch, the king and his ministers, no power to stop public meetings or political writings attacking the government. The government could do nothing to silence government critics unless a judge or jury found the critic guilty of sedition. The law court, not the government, decided what was libel and what was sedition.

The law allowing freedom of the press overturned a century-old custom. From the time of Elizabeth I, the law said that all books and pamphlets had to be registered by the Stationers' Company, those chosen from Parliament to oversee publications. In 1643 Parliament reinforced the law to include approval, which meant censorship. The old law read that no . . . book, pamphlet, paper, nor part of any such . . . shall . . . be printed . . . or put to sale . . . unless the same be first approved and licensed under the hands of such . . . persons as both or either of the . . . Houses shall appoint for the licensing of the same, and entered into the Register Book of the Company of Stationers according to ancient custom.[59]

Authors or printers who violated this law were to be arrested and punished.

The famous English poet John Milton became one of the most outspoken critics of the law. In November 1643, without registering it, he published a pamphlet entitled *Areopagitica* and addressed it to Parliament. (He took the title from Areopagus, the hill where the court of Athens convened.) Milton argued that books are not dead things but are as alive as the souls that created them. He admitted that some books may incite men to arms and other bad things. But he argues that

> he who destroys a good book, kills reason itself, kills the image of God, as it were, in the eye. Many a man lives a burden to the earth; but a good book is the precious life-blood of a master spirit. . . . Revolutions of ages do not oft recover the loss of a rejected truth, for the want of which whole nations fare the worse. We should be wary therefore what persecution we raise against the living labours [books] of public men, how we spill that seasoned life of man, preserved and stored up in books.[60]

Parliament ignored Milton's pamphlet and legislated more severe laws in 1647, 1649, and 1653. Fifty-two years later the Revolution Settlement overturned those censorship laws.

William and Mary as Leaders

William, who took many risks to restore freedom to England's Parliament, began his reign as a popular monarch. He ruled with decency, fairness, and hard work, paying particular attention to England's safety

When the 1695 Parliament overturned censorship laws, it enacted poet John Milton's argument that "he who destroys a good book, kills reason itself."

and power among other nations. Yet, as his reign wore on, he became more and more unpopular because he lacked the social charm Londoners traditionally found important. He became the object of their satire and cartoons. Historian Thomas Babington Macaulay says:

His manners gave almost universal offence. He was in truth far better qualified to save a nation than to adorn a court. In the highest parts of statesmanship, he had no equal among his contemporaries. . . . Fleets and armies, collected to withstand him, had, without a struggle, submitted to his orders. Factions and sects [religious groups], divided by mortal antipathies [enmities], had recognised him as their common head. Without carnage, without devastation, he had won a victory.[61]

But Londoners had enjoyed the gaiety and charm of court life that had surrounded monarchs from the time of Elizabeth I and found the new absence of fashionable society contemptible. Again historian Macaulay offers a perspective:

The Difficulty of Censorship

In his argument opposing censorship, Areopagitica, *John Milton explains the absurdity of employing only twenty licensers in the Stationers' Company to approve and regulate what people can read.*

"If we think to regulate printing, thereby to rectify [correct] manners, we must regulate all recreations and pastimes, all that is delightful to man. No music must be heard, no song be set or sung, but what is grave [serious and moral]. . . . It will ask more than the work of twenty licensers to examine all the lutes, the violins, and the guitars in every house; they must not be suffered [allowed] to prattle as they do, but must be licensed what they may say. And who shall silence all the airs and madrigals [songs] that whisper softness in chambers? The windows also, and the balconies must be thought on; there are shrewd books, with dangerous frontispieces, set to sale; who shall prohibit them, shall twenty licensers? The villages also must have their visitors to inquire what lectures the bagpipe and the rebeck [a medieval instrument with two or three strings] reads, even to the ballatry and the gamut [the whole range of musical notes] of every municipal fiddler. . . . Who shall be the rectors of our daily rioting? . . . Who shall regulate all the mixed conversation of our youth, male and female together, as is the fashion of this country?"

One of the chief functions of our Sovereigns had long been to preside over the society of the capital. . . . [Charles II's] easy bow, his good stories, his style of dancing and playing tennis, the sound of his cordial laugh, were familiar to all London. . . . But of this sociableness William was entirely destitute. He seldom came forth from his closet [private rooms]; and when he appeared in the public rooms, he stood among the crowd of courtiers and ladies, stern and abstracted, making no jest and smiling at none. His freezing look, his silence, the dry and concise answers which he uttered when he could keep silent no longer, disgusted noblemen and gentlemen who had been accustomed to be slapped on the back by their royal masters, called Jack or Harry, congratulated about race cups or rallied about actresses. . . . And they pronounced that this great soldier and politician was no better than a Low Dutch bear.[62]

Though William spoke English, he lacked another quality important to fashionable Londoners—a proper London accent. And he lacked the proper behavior of a tall, distinguished English gentleman. He had asthma, and the smoke and stench of London air made him cough and gasp for air.

Queen Mary, on the other hand, made up for whatever was lacking in her husband's charm. She was English by birth and had a proper English accent and proper English feelings and tastes. Beautiful, majestic, sweet, lively, and quick-witted, she had the feminine charm and shrewdness to please London society. She knew what would please the society's taste and which charities to visit. So assured was

Queen Mary used her charm and grace to win the favor of the English people.

she of her husband's affection that she often used her soft and playful conversation to turn disapproval away from her husband. She did all she could to win English hearts for him. But her reign was cut short; she died of smallpox in December 1694. Her husband reigned until his death in 1702. Of his end, Ariel and Will Durant say:

Domestic Versus Foreign Policy

Godfrey Davies explains the importance William III placed on foreign policy in contrast to the importance Englishmen placed on domestic affairs. The excerpt comes from an essay published in Essays on the Later Stuarts.

"The 'glorious revolution of 1688' created William III and Mary II joint sovereigns of England, Scotland, Ireland, and the colonies, but the administration was lodged in William's hands. His expedition to England had saved constitutional liberties and protestant ascendancy [domination], both endangered by his father-in-law, James II. Yet he had another interest which engrossed him more than these—to join England to the enemies of France. He had been, and continued to be, the mainstay of every coalition to stop Louis XIV from reducing his neighbors to a state of vassalage [servitude]. As one of the most astute of his ministers noted, he was so intent upon an invasion of France that he seemed to have taken England only in his way [become king of England so that he had military power to invade France].

William had to overcome Scottish Jacobites [those still loyal to James II] and Irish nationalists before he could throw the whole weight of England into the scales against France and thus restore the balance of power in Europe. Both tasks were accomplished by 1692. . . . He had already come to believe that Englishmen were absorbed in internal politics, and directed their energies rather to domestic upsets than to farsighted measures to ward off dangers threatened from the outside. Therefore, he was determined to be his own foreign minister."

But when he laid his bent, asthmatic, and tubercular body down to his final rest (March 8, 1702), he could console his domestic defeats with the consciousness that he had at last brought England into resolute participation in the Grand Alliance (1701) which, after twelve years of struggle, would bring the great Bourbon [Louis XIV] to his knees, save the independence of Protestant Europe, and leave England free to spread her power over the world.[63]

Chapter

7 From Ideas to Effects

Seventeenth-century England had two revolutions—one political and the other intellectual. The political revolution brought a change from a constitutional monarchy to a reorganized system of representational government. The intellectual revolution brought a change from absolutist thinking based on authority to thinking based on reason. The two revolutions developed gradually and simultaneously. Both revolutions contributed to the era of peace and prosperity that followed the Glorious Revolution.

Before the seventeenth century, historians Wallbank and Taylor say, "the stream of history flowed its course in the direction of absolutism."[64] Absolutism assumes the world is ordered from above, first from God and then from kings and queens. Absolutists assume that God has planned the world and has power to cause events in it. In regard to monarchs, absolutists assume that monarchs can rule a nation and that their word is beyond question. Absolutism focuses on supernaturalism, a dogmatic, or dictatorial church, God's miracles, divine right, and royal prerogatives. A person with an absolutist outlook will look toward tradition or authority as a source of knowledge. The old way of thinking was grounded in religion; the new way of thinking was grounded in science, mathematics, and experimentation.

The Introduction of Science

English scientist Francis Bacon paved the way for a new philosophy. Bacon was a scholar trained during the reign of Elizabeth. He became a statesman and member of Parliament, holding several positions in the government of James I. Toward the end of his life, he focused his attention on science. He thought that empirical evidence—what a person can observe with the five senses—leads to knowledge. He developed his idea into a scientific method, the practice of observing many particular objects, looking for patterns, and drawing conclusions. For example, if a scientist observes the behavior of many individual squirrels gathering acorns in autumn, eventually the scientist could detect a pattern and draw conclusions about food habits for all squirrels. Bacon published his idea for this scientific method in 1620, in a piece called *Novum Organum, The New Way*. People who read Bacon's work thought that perhaps their own observations could also lead to knowledge and solutions. In a limited way

English scientist Francis Bacon revolutionized scientific thought during the seventeenth century by using empirical inquiry as the basis for discovery.

Bacon's idea began to undermine the belief in absolute authority.

New ways of thinking emerge slowly, and for a long time old and new ways overlap. Oxford historian Alan Chapman relates a story that illustrates how the two kinds of thought could exist at the same time. Scientists at Oxford University used Bacon's scientific method to discover knowledge about the human body. For their observations they were allowed to dissect bodies of criminals after they had been hanged. Anne Green had been hanged on Castle Hill green for murdering a child. Her body was brought to rooms at Carfax Tower, the scientists' laboratory for dissection. Fifteen prominent members of the university prepared for their work when a

rattle came from Anne Green's throat. They gave her brandy, and she came back to life. The hangmen had obviously botched their job. News of the incident spread, and the men in the room were credited with the supernatural power of being able to bring the dead back to life. Scientists, using the new thinking, could observe that Anne Green had never been dead, but people accustomed to the old way of thinking were quick to believe that the scientists' powers came from above.

After a gradual beginning during the first half of the seventeenth century, the scientific method and the reasoning that accompanied it spread rapidly through English society during the second half, especially during the Restoration, the period beginning with the reign of Charles II. The new thinking continued to focus on the world of nature and what could be observed and discovered about it. English physicist Isaac Newton perhaps best represents the new era of science and reason. Newton discovered laws, or principles, by means of reason and mathematics to explain the natural world. In 1687 when James II was England's king, Newton published *Principia Mathematica*, in which he explained laws of nature he had discovered. English poet Alexander Pope illustrates how important Newton's contribution was to the change in thinking when he wrote the humorous couplet: "Nature and nature's laws lay hid by night;/ God said, 'Let Newton be,' and all was light."[65]

Scientific thinking and rational thought spread from scientists in universities to the whole society of educated people. When educated people applied the reasoned methods of scientists to events and social situations surrounding them, they questioned the authority of the king

Isaac Newton's application of the scientific method forever changed the way people view the natural world.

and the church and doubted that absolute allegiance to them was necessarily wise. It would be incorrect to suggest that scientists directly caused the political revolution, but the presence of scientific thought and reason among the leaders affected the way they managed political events.

The Importance of John Locke

One leading scholar of the seventeenth century used the reason of science and applied it to human nature. English philosopher John Locke, who built on the ideas of Francis Bacon, wrote and circulated two essays entitled *Two Treatises on Government*. One was later published in 1689, the year the Glorious Revolution ended, the other in 1690. In these two pieces Locke developed a theory that defined the role of the

government and its relationship to the people. By the time he died in 1704, "his political, philosophical, and religious theories had been absorbed by the English educated classes in an astonishing manner," says Maurice Ashley.[66] Locke said that people were born free and equal and that God had not put any person above another. He wanted to prove that governments are not supreme authorities and can be replaced by society if they violate the principles for which they were established.

Locke set forth his theory of government in a few basic principles. His argument proceeds from one step to the next.

One of Newton's greatest works, Principia Mathematica, *created a profound revolution in scientific thinking by explaining laws of nature as they had never been explained before.*

PHILOSOPHIÆ

NATURALIS

PRINCIPIA

MATHEMATICA.

Autore *JS. NEWTON*, *Trin. Coll. Cantab. Soc.* Matheseos Professore *Lucasiano*, & Societatis Regalis Sodali.

IMPRIMATUR·

S. PEPYS, *Reg. Soc.* PRÆSES.

Julii 5. 1686.

LONDINI,

Jussu *Societatis Regiæ* ac Typis *Josephi Streater*. Prostat apud plures Bibliopolas. *Anno* MDCLXXXVII.

He first said that all people begin in an ordered state of nature that existed before governments. Inherent in nature are people's natural rights, which are the rights to life, liberty, and property. These rights are natural, inalienable—that is, they cannot be transferred to others—and sacred. He argued that the laws of nature are open to differences in interpretation. Consequently, no superior force exists in the world to enforce the laws of nature and to insure that all people have equal opportunity for their rights. Therefore, he rea-

English philosopher John Locke's political theories redefined the role of the government and its relationship to the people.

soned, governments are necessary to maintain the natural laws and to guarantee every person's rights. By common consent people enter into an agreement that a government be set up with the power to govern the people and enforce the laws of nature. When people enter into an agreement to set up a government, they automatically give up some rights, but they do not surrender their natural rights. Finally, the agreement, which establishes an organized society and a government to run it, is bilateral; that is, it is binding on both parties. The government can demand that people obey the laws, but the people can expect the government not to violate their natural rights. If it does, the people have the right to replace it. Thus, the people are indeed the rulers.

Locke's theory puts forth a reasonable argument to justify the Glorious Revolution and to guide the Revolution Settlement. Locke stated in his two treatises, or essays, that a government should have separate legislative (the most important), executive, and judicial branches to serve as a system of checks and balances so that no one part of government acquires too much power. According to historian Maurice Ashley, "Locke's political ideas spread like wildfire."[67] The ideas endured in the philosophy of the governing classes in England for two hundred years, and they were later embedded in the American Constitution.

Peace Brings Prosperity

At the dawn of the eighteenth century, with the Glorious Revolution behind them and with reason to guide them, the En-

The East India Company's fleet leaves port to export English wares to foreign countries.

glish began to experience the benefits of their accomplishments. Their reorganized government brought peace, prosperity, and social and cultural changes.

With peace at home and abroad and with a newly developed system of finances, industry expanded and foreign trade increased. The coal mining industry expanded to provide fuel to heat homes. Manufacturers developed industries in salt, glass, and shipbuilding. Farmers developed a large industry based on barley and sheep. From the sheep industry developed the manufacture of woolen cloth. England had products to export. Trade with foreign countries expanded with the development of trading companies, such as the South Sea Company and the East India Company. Traders, for example, brought woolen cloth to Greece and Spain and returned with currants from Greece and wine from Spain and sold these products for profit. England became a business nation with a growing capitalist class and a growing laborer class. While the gap between rich and poor remained wide, greater prosperity improved the lot of all classes, including the peasants who could, for example, buy more meat and bread. As historian Maurice Ashley says,

"The kingdom had begun to bask in the warmth of a long and victorious peace."[68]

As industry and trade expanded, England developed an empire of colonies around the world. Acquiring colonies had begun in the seventeenth century under the Stuart kings, but it expanded and prospered after the Revolution. The English colonial empire grew to include Bermuda and the West Indies, Newfoundland and Nova Scotia in Canada, India, nearly all of the American colonies, and colonies in Africa. England acquired colonies primarily for economic reasons; the colonies supplied products for England, and the colonies, in turn, became markets for English goods. Precious metals, pepper, spices, timber, tobacco, and sugar were some of the products colonies supplied and English merchants used or sold. Colonialism, however, often exploited the citizens of the colonies. For example, to improve output on the tobacco plantations in the American colonies, merchants imported slaves from Africa and then went on to build a profitable slave trade. Because of the country's fine navy, England became the world's most powerful sea power, an aid in expanding the colonial empire.

Prosperity Brings Social Change

In the atmosphere of prosperity and reason, English society underwent social changes. Attention shifted from religious passion to moral reform. Maurice Ashley said, "These were Christians who set more store upon a decent life than on sacraments and ritual."[69] Because Protestants had more freedom, they were more content. No longer fighting for religious rights, writers and teachers promoted the virtues of decent conduct and reformed manners. While the usual gambling, drinking, prostitution, and bribery still existed, speaking against such behaviors be-

The Use of Economic Freedom

Historian George Macaulay Trevelyan, in The English Revolution 1688–1689, *explains how economic abuses relate to individual freedom.*

"The revolution gave to England an ordered and legal freedom, and through that it gave her power. She often abused her power, as in the matters of Ireland and of the Slave Trade, till she reversed the engines; but on the whole mankind would have breathed a harsher air if England had not grown strong. For her power was based, not only on her free Constitution but on the maritime and commercial enterprise of her sons, a kind of power naturally akin to freedom, as the power of great armies in its nature is not."

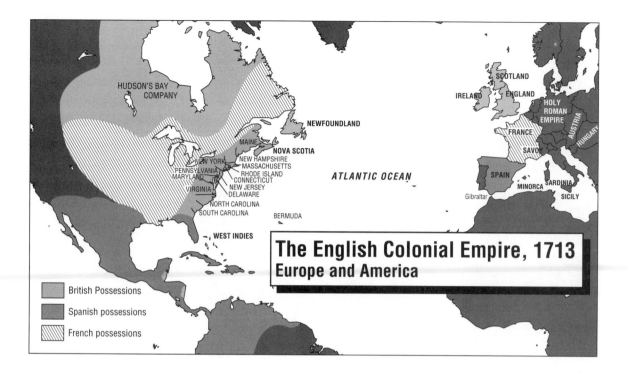

The English Colonial Empire, 1713
Europe and America

British Possessions

Spanish possessions

French possessions

came more openly acceptable. King William himself ordered clergy to preach against blasphemy, swearing, and drunkenness. To bring about moral reform during William's reign, groups formed, such as the Society for the Promotion of Christian Knowledge, the Society for the Propagation of the Gospel, and the Society for the Reforming of Manners.

In addition, the era of prosperity and reason brought humanitarian social changes. Homes were established for the old, disabled, and poor. Many families took in orphans and raised and educated them. For the first time in modern history, an act of international charity occurred when England gave £100,000 to her economic ally, Portugal, to help those who had suffered from the Lisbon earthquake of 1755. In the 125 years following the Revolution, England established 154 new hospitals and health clinics, most of them financed by private persons. Historians Ariel and Will Durant describe one of the charitable projects:

The best of those set up in the first half of the eighteenth century was the Foundling Hospital, organized by Captain Thomas Coram. . . . Coram had earned his fortune as a captain in the merchant marine. Retiring, he was shocked by the high infant mortality [death rate] in London, and by the number of infants exposed or deserted by mothers with no funds to care for them or no father's name to give them. Coram persuaded highborn ladies to sign a petition for a foundling [deserted or abandoned child] hospital; . . . his appeal for contributions was met with unexpected generosity; the great Handel gave an organ and the now precious score of his *Messiah*, and directed concerts that

The prosperity that came to England after the Revolution prompted the rich to display their wealth by wearing elaborate clothing. Men wore powdered wigs, bright coats, and ruffles, while women wore costly dresses and elaborate hairdos.

raised ten thousand pounds. In 1739 the trustees commissioned Theodore Jacobsen to design a spacious group of buildings and grounds, which became one of the proudest sights in London.[70]

Prosperity brought an emphasis on fashion that gave the rich a chance to display their wealth in new styles. Eighteenth-century fashionable men had powdered wigs pulled back with ribbons and wore three-cornered hats. They wore bright-colored, knee-length coats made of rich brocades, or embroidered fabrics, and decorated with buttons and watch fobs. At their necks they wore white ruffled cra-

vats, or ties, of fine imported fabric. Their pants were knee breeches, worn with red or white hose. The rich carried swords, the middle class, canes. There were, however, a few independents who rebelled against the obvious display of wealth. One group, called the Slovens, "made a religion of careless manners and untidy clothes; they disheveled their hair with rebellious care, left their breeches unbuckled, and flaunted the mud on their shoes as declarations of independence and emblems of original thought," report historians Ariel and Will Durant.[71]

Women drew attention to themselves with costly fashion. Popular after the Revolution were fluffy dresses with yards of fabric and wide hoops, some nine yards around. Women elevated their hair in artificial beehive styles topped by pointed hats, so high they had to guard lest they set themselves alight from the candles in the chandeliers. The Durants describe the style: "Feminine faces were concealed by lotions, pastes, patches, powders, and adjustable eyebrows; and all the gems of the Orient were commandeered to adorn their hair and ears and neck and arms and dress and shoes."[72] From their hats to their shoes, women perfumed and designed themselves to attract the attention of men.

So satisfied were the English with the peace and prosperity that they made no changes in the Revolution Settlement until 1829, except to add the office of prime minister and a few new roles for the cabinet. Lest they lose the life they enjoyed, leaders and the people feared reform, and an attitude of conservatism set in. They upheld the letter of the Settlement long after reform was needed to accommodate social changes. When reform did come, the essential features of the constitution established in the Settlement remained the same, but they passed new laws to include the rights of common people.

The English Home

In an age of prosperity, the English home was both a place for escape and another opportunity to display finery. In The Age of Voltaire, *historians Ariel and Will Durant describe the lighting and furnishings found in English homes.*

"Home was a place where one might discard the laborious accouterments [objects] of display; there one could dress in anything or less. Windows were not inquisitive [people peering in], for their number was held down by a law that limited them to five and taxed any surplus as luxury. Interiors were dark and stuffy, and not designed for breathing. Lighting was by candles, usually not more than one at a time per family; the rich, however, brightened their rooms with gleaming chandeliers and with torches burning oil. In the mansions of the well-to-do, walls were paneled in oak, staircases were of massive wood and unshakable balustrades [railings], fireplaces were marbles of majesty, chairs were padded with hair and upholstered in leather. Furniture was designed in heavy 'Georgian' style, complex with carving and glaring with gilt. Toward 1720 mahogany was introduced from the West Indies; it was too hard for existing tools; sharper tools were made; and soon the new wood made the most brilliant pieces in English homes."

Toleration and Individualism

The spirit of toleration, that important attitude that developed when Tories and Whigs decided to live and let others live, brought decades of peace. In his book Spirit of England, *historian Arthur Bryant explains the source for the emerging attitude.*

"This hard-learnt toleration, and all the tolerated eccentricity [behavior different from the usual] arising from it, have rested in the last resort on the Christian belief in the sanctity [sacredness] of the individual. . . . At its core lay the thesis that every man, being free to choose between good and evil, was a soul of equal value in the eyes of God. It was this which gave rise to an Englishman's saying in the English revolution of the seventeenth century that the 'poorest he in England hath a life to live as the greatest he.'. . .

The virtues of England sprang from nature, but also from conscious will. The English were what they were because deep down they wished to be. Their tradition derived from their ancient Catholic past. Its purpose at its highest was to make Christian men; gentle, generous, humble, valiant, and chivalrous. Its enduring ideals were justice, mercy, and charity. Shakespeare was not writing fantasy when he put into the mouth of John of Gaunt his vision of a

Land of such dear souls, this dear, dear land:
Dear for her reputation through the world,

he was merely defining the idealised character of his country."

Unlike America, England has never had a written constitution. England's constitution has always been the country's laws and the country's tradition of valuing individual liberty and obeying the law. According to a recent letter to the *New York Times*, there is today a growing movement for a written constitution. The movement originated because some people saw individual rights eroding. The movement aims to "restore liberty and entrench it for the first time in Britain with a democratic written constitution. Charter 88 is perhaps its leading proponent. Founded on the tricentenary [three-hundredth anniversary] of the 'Glorious Revolution' of 1688, it protested that 300 years of unwritten rule was enough."[73] For those who lived during the century right after the Revolution, however, their unwritten constitution was all they could have hoped it would be.

From England to the World

Seldom in history has an event of such short duration and enacted with so little drama had such a deep and widespread meaning as the Glorious Revolution has had. England led the way with the first revolution of its kind. Though the Glorious Revolution itself was bloodless, England had paid a heavy price in suffering and abuses for nearly a century before it. The reorganized government of the Revolution Settlement became the model for representative government in Europe and America and in countries throughout the world. Its ideas and practices embedded themselves first in the minds of the English and then in the minds of people in all established democracies. These ideals remain the goals for people in countries still striving for representative government.

Observing the success in England after the Revolution, European philosophers turned against political despotism and religious intolerance because they could see that those practices weakened their own countries. European leaders could see that England's parliamentary government operated more efficiently and fairly than governments in other countries. Within a century many countries had taken action to accomplish change. In 1776 America had a revolution and established a new government, and in 1789 France had one.

Neither, however, was accomplished without bloodshed as the Glorious Revolution had been.

The American Revolution

Besides the English people, none have benefited from the Glorious Revolution more than Americans. Less than a century after the Revolution, American colonies revolted against England and declared themselves a nation with the right to their own government. The colonies revolted, not because they hated English government, but because they wanted to be governed with the same rights as the English were governed. In other words, Americans revolted against abuses of the government, not the government itself.

After a successful revolution the American founding fathers used the political philosophy of John Locke and the English model developed during the Settlement as a basis for their new democracy. Because the founding fathers could benefit from England's decades of conflicts and violence, they made changes in the English model when they wrote the American Constitution. For example, after all the problems with religions, Americans made

In an act of defiance, Americans pull down the statue of King George, demanding to be governed by the same rights as the English.

the separation of the church and the state a part of the Constitution from the beginning. Americans have also incorporated many of the institutions developed by the English. Again, Americans have modified details. America has all the institutions developed during the Settlement, a two-party system, a cabinet, civil control of the military, free press, and capitalism. Historian J. R. Jones says, "Today everyone in Britain and the United States is in a sense a residuary beneficiary of [benefiting from what remained after] the Revolution."[74]

The principles of the Revolution have become deeply embedded in the English national character to the degree that they have become habits. "Long use and cus-

tom have made liberty and peaceful self-government natural to Englishmen," says historian Trevelyan.[75] The Revolution was a victory for moderation, for the art of leaving one another alone, and for respecting individualism; it was a defeat for fanaticism, meddling, and domination. Because three centuries ago the English were set free to worship and to speak and write as they pleased, they are still free, and the freedoms are a habit. But the years before the Revolution had also taught them that liberty does not thrive in an atmosphere of force and disorder; consequently, they came to cherish the framework of discipline in which freedom can thrive. That framework is the law. Historian Arthur Bryant says, "This respect for the law gradually made the English people, who might otherwise have been one of the most difficult to govern, one of the easiest: easy, that is, so long as they are governed lawfully. It became habitual to obey the law and see it enforced."[76] Because government by law is so deeply entrenched in the national character, English government can remain stable and right itself again if wars or crises or scandals disrupt it.

These same habits of thought have also become embedded in the minds of Americans and all people in well-established democracies, whose governments also can withstand wars, natural disasters, and political campaigns. Those countries with a long history of democracy sometimes fail to remember how difficult it was to begin. Several English historians think it lucky that England had its revolution first a long time ago. The nation has had the time to let "compromise, give-and-take, live-and-let-live . . . become a national habit. . . . Without justice and charity there could be no England. That has remained, and remains, the historic and unchanging English vision" and the vision of millions of others.[77]

Notes

Introduction: The Struggles for Power and Religious Freedom

1.   Maurice Ashley, *The Glorious Revolution of 1688*. New York: Charles Scribner's Sons, 1966, p. 9.

Chapter 1: From Tudor Harmony to Stuart Conflict, 1603–1640

2.   Maurice Ashley, *England in the Seventeenth Century*. 1952. Reprint, New York: Barnes and Noble, 1980, p. 51.

3.   William McElwee, *The Wisest Fool in Christendom: The Reign of King James I and VI*. New York: Harcourt, Brace, 1958, p. 179.

4.   Will Durant and Ariel Durant, *The Age of Reason Begins*. Vol. VII of *The Story of Civilization*. New York: Simon and Schuster, 1961, p. 139.

5.   Ashley, *England in the Seventeenth Century*, p. 63.

6.   Durant and Durant, *The Age of Reason Begins*, pp. 160–161.

7.   Thomas Babington Macaulay, *The History of England from the Accession of James II*. vol. 1. Chicago and New York: Belford, Clarke, 1884, p. 85.

8.   Durant and Durant, *The Age of Reason Begins*, p. 200.

9.   Ashley, *England in the Seventeenth Century*, p. 64.

Chapter 2: From Civil War to Anarchy, 1640–1660

10.   Ashley, *England in the Seventeenth Century*, pp. 88–89.

11.   Quoted in Hugh Ross Williamson, *The Day They Killed the King*. New York: Macmillan, 1957, pp. 25 and 21.

12.   Quoted in Williamson, *The Day They Killed the King*, p. 46.

13.   Williamson, *The Day They Killed the King*, p. 55.

14.   Williamson, *The Day They Killed the King*, p. 142.

15.   Quoted in Williamson, *The Day They Killed the King*, p. 146.

16.   Quoted in Williamson, *The Day They Killed the King*, p. 147.

17.   Ashley, *England in the Seventeenth Century*, pp. 102–103.

Chapter 3: From Restoration to Disarray, 1660–1685

18.   Samuel Pepys, "From *The Diary*," in *English Literature and Its Backgrounds*. Rev. ed. Vol. 1. Edited by Bernard D. Grebanier et al. New York: Dryden Press, 1949, p. 708.

19.   Will Durant and Ariel Durant, *The Age of Louis XIV*. Vol. VIII of *The Story of Civilization*. New York: Simon and Schuster, 1963, p. 224.

20.   Quoted in Godfrey Davies, *Essays on the Later Stuarts*. San Marino, CA: Huntington Library, 1958, p. 18.

21.   Macaulay, *The History of England*, vol. 1, p. 161.

22.   Davies, *Essays on the Later Stuarts*, p. 38.

23.   T. Walter Wallbank and Alastair M. Taylor, *From the Beginnings of the Modern Era to the Present Time*. Vol. 2 of *Civilization: Past and Present*. Chicago: Scott, Foresman, 1949, p. 117.

24.   Macaulay, *The History of England*, vol. 1, p. 161.

25.   Macaulay, *The History of England*, vol. 1, p. 160.

26. Durant and Durant, *The Age of Louis XIV*, p. 249.

27. Ashley, *England in the Seventeenth Century*, p. 133.

28. Wallbank and Taylor, *From the Beginnings*, p. 118.

29. Macaulay, *The History of England*, vol. 1, pp. 220–221.

Chapter 4: From Absolutism to Rebellion, 1685–1688

30. Davies, *Essays on the Later Stuarts*, pp. 44–45.

31. George Macaulay Trevelyan, *The English Revolution 1688–1689*. New York: Henry Holt, 1939, pp. 62–63.

32. Macaulay, *The History of England*, vol. 1, p. 593.

33. Ashley, *England in the Seventeenth Century*, p. 178.

34. J. R. Jones, *The Revolution of 1688 in England*. New York: W. W. Norton, 1972, p. 55.

35. Ashley, *The Glorious Revolution*, pp. 43–44.

36. Quoted in Trevelyan, *The English Revolution*, p. 63.

37. Jones, *The Revolution*, p. 76.

38. Trevelyan, *The English Revolution*, p. 72.

39. Macaulay, *The History of England*, vol. 1, p. 595.

40. Trevelyan, *The English Revolution*, p. 97.

41. Ashley, *The Glorious Revolution*, p. 134.

42. Trevelyan, *The English Revolution*, p. 117.

Chapter 5: From Invasion to Rights, 1688–1689

43. Quoted in Ashley, *The Glorious Revolution*, p. 147.

44. Jones, *The Revolution*, p. 281.

45. Quoted in Jones, *The Revolution*, p. 231.

46. Jones, *The Revolution*, p. 253.

47. Quoted in Ashley, *The Glorious Revolution*, p. 156.

48. Ashley, *The Glorious Revolution*, p. 157.

49. Trevelyan, *The English Revolution*, p. 123.

50. Ashley, *The Glorious Revolution*, p. 177.

51. Trevelyan, *The English Revolution*, pp. 145–146.

52. Quoted in Trevelyan, *The English Revolution*, pp. 157–158.

53. Quoted in Jones, *The Revolution*, p. 319.

54. Jones, *The Revolution*, p. 3.

Chapter 6: From Rights to Settlement, 1689–1702

55. Trevelyan, *The English Revolution*, pp. 180–181.

56. Trevelyan, *The English Revolution*, p. 166.

57. Trevelyan, *The English Revolution*, p. 187.

58. Trevelyan, *The English Revolution*, p. 185.

59. Quoted in Durant and Durant, *The Age of Louis XIV*, p. 224.

60. John Milton, *Areopagitica (the 1644 Text)*. Edited by Israel Gollancz. London: J. M. Dent and Sons, n.d. Reprinted in *Areopagitica and Other Tracts*. Boston: Beacon Press, 1951, pp. 7–8.

61. Macaulay, *The History of England*, vol. 3, pp. 54–55.

62. Macaulay, *The History of England*, vol. 3, pp. 56–57.

63. Durant and Durant, *The Age of Louis XIV*, p. 305.

Chapter 7: From Ideas to Effects

64. Wallbank and Taylor, *From the Beginnings*, p. 115.

65. Quoted in Chapman, lecture 13 of "The English and European Origins of American Culture" series for the Moorhead State University Oxford Study Tour, Oxford, UK, June 1984.

66. Ashley, *England in the Seventeenth Century*, p. 249.

67. Ashley, *England in the Seventeenth Century*, p. 251.

68. Ashley, *England in the Seventeenth Century*, p. 240.

69. Ashley, *England in the Seventeenth Century*, p. 246.

70. Will Durant and Ariel Durant, *The Age of Voltaire*. Vol. IX of *The Story of Civilization*. New York: Simon and Schuster, 1965, p. 69.

71. Durant and Durant, *The Age of Voltaire*, p. 75.

72. Durant and Durant, *The Age of Voltaire*, p. 76.

73. Anthony Barnett, "It's Time Britain Had a Written Constitution," *New York Times*, December 3, 1994, editorial page.

Epilogue: From England to the World

74. Jones, *The Revolution*, p. 8.

75. Trevelyan, *The English Revolution*, p. 218.

76. Arthur Bryant, *Spirit of England*. London: Collins, 1982, p. 45.

77. Bryant, *Spirit of England*, pp. 45 and 47.

For Further Reading

Maurice Ashley, *Great Britain to 1688*. Ann Arbor: University of Michigan Press, 1961. A history divided into four books. Book III describes the Reformation and the reign of Elizabeth I; Book IV tells about economics, social life, education, culture, music, and science during the reigns of the four Stuart kings. Easy reading.

G. E. Aylmer, *A Short History of Seventeenth-Century England*. New York: Mentor Books, 1963. A good explanation of the workings of the government and the causes of conflicts. More emphasis on the civil war than the Glorious Revolution. A chart at the end allows the reader to compare political events, foreign policy, social and religious events, and developments in art and science during a given year.

Charles Blitzer and the Editors of Time-Life Books, *Age of Kings*. Alexandria, VA: Time-Life Books, 1967. Explains life under rule of kings. A separate section shows the struggle between the English Crown and Parliament and includes a photo essay of English life during the era of Samuel Pepys.

Elizabeth Burton, *The Pageant of Elizabethan England*. New York: Charles Scribner's Sons, 1958. Tells about homes, furnishings, food, entertainment, gardens, and women's makeup. Abundantly illustrated with black-and-white drawings.

John Cannon and Ralph Griffiths, *The Oxford Illustrated History of the British Monarchy*. New York: Oxford University Press, 1988. Contains sections on Henry VIII, Elizabeth I, the four Stuarts, and William and Mary. Illustrations include many color photos of the paintings of the times.

Charles Carlton, *Charles I: The Personal Monarch*. London: Routledge & Kegan Paul, 1983. A new interpretation of Charles I based on recent knowledge of history and psychology. Tells about the childhood difficulties Charles I had with his father.

Leonard W. Cowie, *The Trial and Execution of Charles I*. New York: G. P. Putnam's Sons, 1972. Tells about Charles I from the time before the civil war through his execution. Abundantly illustrated with pictures showing Charles in battle, Charles awaiting execution, and Charles on the scaffold.

Roger Hart, *English Life in the Seventeenth Century*. New York: G. P. Putnam's Sons, 1970. A book of drawings, several per page, of people and scenes of the time. Portrays fashion, warfare, houses, street sweepers, weavers, the Great Fire, coffeehouses, and much more.

J. P. Kenyon, *Stuart England*. New York: St. Martin's Press, 1978. A history of England from a poor nation to a major power, written by a working historian. Explains the development of English government and institutions. An easy-to-read book with a good annotated bibliography.

Dirsty McLeod, *Drums and Trumpets: The House of Stuart*. New York: Seabury Press, 1977. Portrays life in country villages and in London during the reigns of the first two Stuarts and emphasizes court life during the reigns of the last Stuarts and William and Mary. Contains many drawings and paintings from the time.

Jean Plaidy, *Gay Lord Robert*. New York: G. P. Putnam's Sons, 1955. A historical novel about the love between Queen Elizabeth I and Robert Dudley, earl of Leicester, the most powerful man during her reign. Portrays the queen as a shrewd and charming woman.

————, *A Health unto His Majesty*. New York: G. P. Putnam's Sons, 1972. A romantic novel about London's social life after Puritan rule. Portrays Charles II through the eyes of his wife and one of his mistresses. Also provides background on the plague, the London fire, and people of the time, such as Titus Oates.

Anne Somerset, *Ladies in Waiting: From the Tudors to the Present Day*. New York: Knopf, 1984. An account of individual ladies-in-waiting, women who surrounded the monarch in the British court. As women during much of the period had no jobs, these women exerted influence because they had titles. The book portrays manners, morals, and philosophies of the rich and famous.

George Macaulay Trevelyan, *The Age of Shakespeare and the Stuart Period*. Vol. 2 of *Illustrated English Social History*. London: Longmans, Green, 1950. Abundant color photos and black-and-white drawings enrich a text that portrays the homes, social classes, education, work, sports, and entertainment of the seventeenth century.

————, *The Tudors and the Stuart Era*. Vol. 2 of *The History of England*. 1926. Reprint, Garden City, NY: Doubleday, 1953. Covers the Tudors through the Revolution Settlement. Explains historical and political events, foreign policy, important ministers, and acts and laws and also shows how these elements reflected change during the century.

Works Consulted

Maurice Ashley, *England in the Seventeenth Century*. 1952. Reprint, New York: Barnes and Noble, 1980. An account of scientific and philosophical ideas and social and cultural life, with emphasis on the political history presented as a chronology of the nation's kings and queens.

——, *The Glorious Revolution of 1688*. New York: Charles Scribner's Sons, 1966. A readable history, beginning with the exclusion issue during the last years of the reign of Charles II. Focuses on causes of the Revolution and motives of James and William. Appendix contains copies of documents.

Anthony Barnett, "It's Time Britain Had a Written Constitution," *New York Times*, December 3, 1994. An opinion by the coordinator of a group called Charter 88 that eroding rights makes a written constitution necessary.

Arthur Bryant, *Spirit of England*. London: Collins, 1982. An English historian's definition of England's special spirit and an analysis of its source in themes that unite the people, such as love of liberty, respect for law, and fondness for the monarchy.

Alan Chapman, "The English and European Origins of American Culture." A series of twenty lectures for the Moorhead State University Oxford Study Tour, Oxford, UK, June 1984. A survey of people and events that influenced England in the sixteenth and seventeenth centuries and influenced the origins of America as a nation.

Godfrey Davies, *Essays on the Later Stuarts*. San Marino, CA: Huntington Library, 1958. Three biographical essays explaining how Charles II, James II, and William III influenced events surrounding the Glorious Revolution.

Will Durant and Ariel Durant, *The Age of Louis XIV*. Vol. VIII of *The Story of Civilization*. New York: Simon and Schuster, 1963. Besides French history, this volume covers English history from Cromwell through the Glorious Revolution, providing social and intellectual history along with political events.

——, *The Age of Reason Begins*. Vol. VII of *The Story of Civilization*. New York: Simon and Schuster, 1961. Besides covering histories of several European countries, this volume gives a lively account of Elizabethan England and the reigns of James I and Charles I. Special chapters explain the development of science and the arts of the time, especially Shakespeare's work.

——, *The Age of Voltaire*. Vol. IX of *The Story of Civilization*. New York: Simon and Schuster, 1965. A volume particularly focused on the intellectual and religious changes during the first half of the eighteenth century, with an extensive section devoted to the developments in England.

David Hume, *The History of England from the Invasion of Julius Caesar to the Revolution in 1688*, new ed., vol. 6. London: A. Strahan, 1802. Based primarily on the daily journal of the House of Commons, this volume offers a detailed account of the politics during the reigns of James I and Charles I.

J. R. Jones, *The Revolution of 1688 in England*. New York: W. W. Norton, 1972. In a new interpretation, Jones presents the Glorious Revolution as more important than the civil war and less inevitable than most historians have considered it to be.

Thomas Babington Macaulay, *The History of England from the Accession of James II*. Chicago and New York: Belford, Clarke, 1884. A lively, well-written, and detailed account of the personalities and events that influenced English history from the time before the Restoration through the reign of William and Mary.

William McElwee, *The Wisest Fool in Christendom: The Reign of King James I and VI*. New York: Harcourt, Brace, 1958. This biography gives a background of James I's Scottish history and the changing England that he ruled. From it comes a better understanding of all the Stuart kings and their part in the events leading to the Glorious Revolution.

John Milton, *Areopagitica (the 1644 Text)*. Edited by Israel Gollancz. London: J. M. Dent and Sons, n.d. Reprinted in *Areopagitica and Other Tracts*. Boston: Beacon Press, 1951. This famous argument for freedom of the press emphasizes the sanctity of contributions made by human souls. Milton argues that control of these contributions is ludicrous.

Samuel Pepys, "From *The Diary*," in *English Literature and Its Backgrounds*. Rev. ed. Vol. 1. Edited by Bernard D. Grebanier et al. New York: Dryden Press, 1949. An eyewitness account of the great events and people of Pepys's time, written with detail in a lively style.

George Macaulay Trevelyan, *The English Revolution 1688–1689*. New York: Henry Holt, 1939. Written by a noted British historian. Covers reigns of Charles II and James II, the Revolution, and the Settlement. Offers good commentary on the meaning of the Revolution and the English spirit.

T. Walter Wallbank and Alastair M. Taylor, *From the Beginnings of the Modern Era to the Present Time*. Vol. 2 of *Civilization: Past and Present*. Chicago: Scott, Foresman, 1949. A broad survey of each era, with a focus on political, economic, and intellectual history.

———, *Paleolithic Era to 1650 A.D.* Vol. 1 of *Civilization: Past and Present*. Chicago: Scott, Foresman, 1949. A broad survey covering a long period, with a focus on cultural development and the religious, political, and military events that shaped the changes.

Hugh Ross Williamson, *The Day They Killed the King*. New York: Macmillan, 1957. A fascinating version of the last days of Charles I: what he ate, what he said, who was with him. The author presents a sympathetic view of the king.

Index

Picture Credits

About the Author

After several years of teaching British literature, Clarice Swisher now devotes her time to research and writing. She is the author of *The Beginning of Language, Relativity, Albert Einstein, Pablo Picasso,* and *The Ancient Near East.* She lives in Saint Paul, Minnesota.